Assistive Technologies
IN THE LIBRARY

Assistive Technologies

IN THE LIBRARY

Barbara T. Mates

WITH CONTRIBUTIONS BY WILLIAM R. REED IV

American Library Association
Chicago   2011

Retiring after twenty-five years as the head of the Ohio Library for the Blind and Physically Disabled, **Barbara T. Mates** now works as an independent consultant specializing in topics related to senior services and accessibility options for persons with disabilities. She is a past president of ALA's Association for Specialized and Cooperative Library Agencies (ASCLA) and chaired ALA's 2010 Schneider Family Book Award Committee. Mates has presented numerous papers and workshops across the country and is the author of 5-Star Programming and Services for Your 55+ Library Customers (ALA, 2003); "Computer Technologies to Aid Special Audiences" (Library Technology Reports, 2004); and "Assistive Technologies for Today's Libraries" (American Libraries, 2010). Her awards include the 2001 Francis Joseph Campbell Award and the 2010 ASCLA Exceptional Service Award.

Printed in the United States of America
15 14 13 12 11   5 4 3 2 1

While extensive effort has gone into ensuring the reliability of the information in this book, the publisher makes no warranty, express or implied, with respect to the material contained herein.

ISBN: 978-0-8389-1070-2

Library of Congress Cataloging-in-Publication Data
Mates, Barbara T.
Assistive technologies in the library / Barbara T. Mates ; with contributions by William R. Reed, IV.
        p.   cm.
   Includes bibliographical references and index.
   ISBN 978-0-8389-1070-2 (alk. paper)
   1. Libraries and people with disabilities. 2. Self-help devices for people with disabilities 3. Libraries and people with visual disabilities. 4. Libraries and the hearing impaired. I. Reed, William R. II. Title.
   Z711.92.H3M323 2011
   027.6'63--dc22
                                                                    2010038258

Book design in Melior and Morgan Office by Kirstin Krutsch.
♾ This paper meets the requirements of ANSI/NISO Z39.48-1992 (Permanence of Paper).

ALA Editions also publishes its books in a variety of electronic formats.
For more information, visit the ALA Store at www.alastore.ala.org and select eEditions.

Contents

This book is dedicated to my parents, Ann Trask and the late Tony Trask, who made sure I received a quality education; and to my husband, James, who provides me unconditional love and understanding; and to my dearest friends, who listen to me but do not judge me—I love you all!

Preface

As *Assistive Technologies in the Library* was being created, many libraries around the world were feeling the crunch of one of the deepest recessions of the last two generations. Administrators and library boards were being forced to rethink their vision and mission statements as well as rework their long- and short-term plans to accommodate funding cutbacks. The number crunchers are still carefully going through libraries' budgets to see where money can be found. Very often they look to see what would do the least harm to the public or what can be eliminated that no one will notice. They look to see which branches can have their hours reduced or staff trimmed. They look to see what services are being underutilized or not utilized. It is when quantitative analysis without qualitative input transpires that services to patrons who need libraries the most are affected. There is a tendency to trim outreach services as well as those services that require a large amount of staff time.

Very often the services that are scaled back are those services to persons with disabilities, as their library use numbers are often low in comparison to those patrons without disabilities. The availability of assistive technologies or an accessible website is not something that is acknowledged by the library profession. Hennen's widely respected index, which ranks U.S.

public libraries, examines "traditional data for print services, book check-outs, reference service, funding and staffing" but does not factor in equity in access to these services.[1]

More than likely, if the library has an extra thousand dollars to spend, and staff can either buy fifty DVDs to circulate or one piece of adaptive software to be used in-house, the DVDs are going to be the selection, as they have the potential to generate ten thousand circulations. This tendency is unfortunate, as people with disabilities are a population that is generally at an economic disadvantage as well as an educational disadvantage and that can benefit the most from free access to technology.

The number of persons with disabilities is also growing as the baby boomers age and as disabilities that cannot be remedied by today's medical advances develop. This, unlike previous generations, is a population that will be demanding access; it is best to be prepared.

Higher numbers of persons with disabilities are also caused by a rise in people with cognitive or learning disorders. Testing mechanisms are allowing professionals to diagnose learning differences as well as autism spectrum disorders in certain of their clients more readily than they had been able to do in the past. As a result, more individuals are realizing that they can be helped by adaptive technologies to reach their own achievement goals.

Although there is a venerable network in place—the National Library Service for the Blind and Physically Handicapped (a division of the Library of Congress), which provides materials for leisure reading for some people with disabilities—there is now a growing need for access to information and technology within the individuals' communities.[2] As with the general population, people with disabilities need to be able to access the Internet to research benefits, identify local community resources, download books and music, learn, and grow.

Assistive Technologies in the Library seeks to guide information providers in selecting technologies, designing accessible websites, learning how to purchase accessible electronic resources, establishing access policies, training staff to work with patrons with disabilities, funding accessible technologies, and marketing the services using both traditional methods and new social networking tools.

This book incorporates work (chapters 2 and 12) by William R. Reed IV, the regional librarian for the Ohio Library for the Blind and Physically Disabled. He has worked with the American Library Association to ensure that members of the association with disabilities can access the ALA site. Additionally, he led a task force to develop a checklist to which persons making purchasing decisions can refer to determine if a resource is accessible. He represents the generation of librarians who will develop methods to help people with disabilities exploit electronic resources.

Within *Assistive Technologies in the Library,* information providers will be given the tools to develop and retain access in their libraries, and they will learn how to convince their financial personnel that it would be more expensive not to create accessibility portals in the library than to create them. A population that is gainfully employed and educated has a greater tendency to vote for library levies. It is my hope that this work will enable all libraries to give all patrons equal access to information and services.

Notes

1. For further information on Hennen's American Public Library Rating Index, visit www.haplr-index.com/faq.html.
2. The National Library Service for the Blind and Physically Handicapped, part of the Library of Congress, provides books and magazines on cassette tape, in Braille, and in digital cartridge format to qualified patrons in the United States and its territories; visit www.loc.gov/nls/.

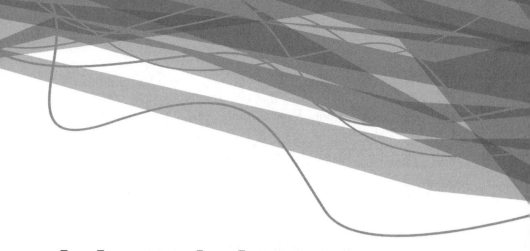

Acknowledgments

Kindness is a language which the deaf can hear and the blind can read.
—Mark Twain

Books are composed of many words, concepts, and ideas and often only carry the imprint of the person(s) who physically wrote the book. But in actuality, books are the sum of many others. This book is no exception. Therefore, allow me to share with and thank those who are also part of this book.

I thank my friends and colleagues within the American Library Association (ALA), the Association for Specialized and Cooperative Library Agencies (ASCLA), and Libraries Serving Special Populations Section (LSSPS), who enabled me to find answers to access issues with which I was unfamiliar. All of you are true professionals and appreciated by both the patrons you serve and your colleagues alike. I especially thank William R. Reed IV for his contributions to ALA as part of the Web Accessibility Committee and for leading an ad hoc committee for librarians to use when crafting accessible websites and purchasing electronic databases.

I thank my former patrons, who made me realize the need for access to information. Witnessing your frustrations and your triumphs encouraged me to advocate for your right to use your local library and access information. I also thank those persons with disabilities whom I consider my friends, such as Nichole Maples, Max Edelman, and the "Roses," for providing me with additional motivation.

I especially thank Irwin Hott, a former patron, for willingly reading some of the chapters for me and ensuring that I got the terminology correct.

I also thank Orene Anthony, also a former patron, for writing the poem "SOME Difference" and allowing me to include it in this work. The poem succinctly addresses why I work to promote access to information for all people.

I thank all the contact people at assistive-technology websites for responding to questions promptly and positively. I especially thank the folks at ULVA, in Columbus, Ohio. All of you have been so knowledgeable and supportive over the years and made the adding of assistive technologies stress-free.

I thank front-line librarians and those in administrative positions who listen to patrons and their advocates and approve the spending of dollars in regard to ensuring equity in access. Your dedication enables people with disabilities to cross the digital divide. I especially thank Jo Budler, Wisconsin State Librarian (and former State Librarian in Ohio), for working to make virtual library services, such as KnowItNow 24x7, accessible.

I thank the multitude of organizations, schools, and individuals who work tirelessly and often without appropriate financial remuneration to create access tools and guidelines that allow persons with disabilities to use computers and have full lives.

I thank my husband, James, for proofreading the work, taking the pictures, and making the tables. Once again, a job well done.

I thank ALA editor Stephanie Zvirin for asking me to update *Adaptive Technology for the Internet* (2000). I welcome the opportunity to update readers on the multitude of advancements in the assistive-technology arena.

I also want to thank the copy editors and layout editors at ALA Editions who made this work look good.

Finally, I would like to thank Eloise Kinney for doing such a great job of editing this book—I truly appreciate every hyphen she added and every *assure* she corrected.

1
The Library's Mission
To Serve All Patrons

There are some staff members and administrators who think that their library does not have any people in their service area with disabilities because they do not see any in the library. The truth of the matter is that people with disabilities live, love, and learn everywhere. There are no ghettos of people with disabilities, and unless these libraries are in an alternate reality, they need to examine the reasons why they are not seeing people with disabilities using their library.

Statistics

Determining accurate statistics of persons with disabilities is a difficult task, as the term *disability* is totally subjective on the part of the person being queried. For example, a person whose vision is so limited that she must be three inches from a monitor may feel that her vision is not a disability, as she can still read the text on the screen. She would probably reply in the negative to the question of whether she had a disability. Likewise, someone who has severe arthritis in her hands might not think of herself as having a disability, while another person with recurrent calluses on her hands would say she has a disability. This reaction replays itself throughout the disability spectrum. Yet here's just one piece of data worth noting as the library does long-range planning: experts predict that by 2030, rates of vision loss will double along with the country's aging population.[1]

Researchers and census takers all agree that the total number of people with disabilities is very large, and probably larger than is being reported. Some interesting statistics include those from the World Health Organization, which estimates that of the world's population of 6.5 billion people, nearly 100 million are moderately or severely disabled.[2] According to the U.S. Census Bureau, as of 2004 there were some 32 million disabled adults (aged eighteen or over) in the United States, plus another 5 million disabled children and youth (under age eighteen).[3] If one were to add impairments or limitations that fall short of being disabilities, the census estimates put the figure at 51 million.[4] These numbers make Americans with disabilities the third-largest minority (after persons of Hispanic origin and African Americans); all three of those minority groups number over 30 million Americans.[5] Yet the amount of dollars spent by libraries or other institutions to remove barriers and offer services to Americans with disabilities is well below its proportion in the population.

Although there are not overall, definite disability statistics, those related to vision loss are more reliable. This can be attributed to organizations such as the American Foundation for the Blind (AFB), which has excellent data collection and research facilities. The AFB maintains a user-friendly facts-and-figures database that can be accessed by state.[6] This data should be helpful when determining what types of software and hardware to purchase.

Laws Relating to Access for Persons with Disabilities

It is important to be aware of laws that govern access to information for persons with disabilities, as failure to comply may result in cause for litigation. Applicable laws are Sections 504 and 508 of the Rehabilitation Act of 1973 and the Americans with Disabilities Act (ADA) of 1990, which was amended in 2008 and reaffirmed in 2009.[7] Section 8 of the "Americans with Disabilities Act Accessibility Guidelines" (ADAAG) specifically addresses libraries.

Briefly, these laws mandate that persons with disabilities have access to public programs and services. Thus, if the library offers free access to computers and training, it must offer access for persons who need adapted access avenues. Reasonable accommodations must also be made to meet the needs of staff with disabilities.

ALA Takes a Positive Stand on Accessibility for All

The American Library Association (ALA) has long held that libraries were places where people could access and exchange information in a manner that was undeterred by predisposed policies and barriers. The ALA "Mission Statement" states that the work of the association and libraries is "to ensure access to information and enhance learning and ensure access to information for all," and the preamble to the Library Bill of Rights clarifies that "all libraries are forums for information and ideas."[8]

In 2008, the ALA offered an interpretation of this Bill of Rights as it applies to persons with disabilities. In part it reads: "ALA recognizes that persons with disabilities are a large and often neglected part of society. In addition to many personal challenges, some persons with disabilities face economic inequity, illiteracy, cultural isolation, and discrimination in education, employment, and the broad range of societal activities. The library plays a catalytic role in their lives by facilitating their full participation in society."[9]

Universal Access through Universal Design

If the library is in the fortuitous position of undergoing a major renovation or undertaking a new building project, then the best approach for creating an environment that all people can use is to apply "universal design" principles. Universal design was defined by the late architect Ron Mace as "the concept of designing all products and the built environment to be aesthetic and usable to the greatest extent possible by everyone, regardless of their age, ability, or status in life."[10] The intent of universal design is to simplify life for everyone by making products, communications, and the built environment more usable by as many people as possible at little or no extra cost. Universal design benefits people of all ages and abilities.[11]

Universal design in learning environments can be accomplished by providing multiple means of representation, action, expression, and engagement. Through thoughtful planning and without spending additional money, the library can create an environment in which a person with or without a disability feels comfortable. Universal design can save money by not having to make adaptations or accommodations. Additionally, there is the bonus to patrons, as there isn't a stigma attached to having to have accommodations made for their disability. Examples of this concept would be a ramp entrance to a building, where steps would traditionally be placed, that would accommodate wheelchairs as well as strollers; adjustable work-stations throughout the facility; and clear signage that could be read and comprehended.

The concept of universal design also extends to the virtual library site as well. If web pages are designed correctly, persons using screen readers will be able to access the pages unassisted; people with cognitive disabilities will be able to understand the text without needing translations. This flexibility also benefits people *without* disabilities in certain situations, such as people using a slow Internet connection, people with "temporary disabilities" such as a broken arm, and people with changing abilities caused by aging.[12] Thoughtful design once again saves staff from constantly being queried needlessly; plus, it empowers the user through independence.

Assistive Technologies Help Everyone

Younger people may not remember a time when street crossings did not have curb cuts in them, but such a time did exist. If one was using a wheel-chair, crossing the street unassisted was virtually impossible without risking injury to self or to chair. As city planners actually started renovations, they found that the Americans with Disabilities Act mandated curb cuts; they complied with the mandates, and curb cuts became a way of life. In addition to people using wheelchairs or scooters using curb cuts, businesspeople with wheeled bags use them, as do parents with strollers, people on skateboards, and people riding bicycles. Curb cuts are used instinctively by the mass population, as they make moving about easier.

Likewise, some of the assistive technologies that are added to the library environment are used by people without disabilities. In a survey conducted by Microsoft, it was determined that 57 percent of computer users would benefit from the use of accessible technology.[13] Oversize monitors are sought out by many, as it's just easier to see what is displayed; trackballs help some patrons scroll through large amounts of text more quickly; tables that have the ability to be raised or lowered help patrons who may just be having a physically hard day and need to sit differently.

Adaptations you make for patrons with special needs do have the potential for serving more patrons than those they are intended to aid. If you only have funding for one computer station, make it one that will serve all patrons.

Brave New World via the Computer and Internet

Computers and the Internet have become a necessity for many. For those with disabilities, these technologies have an even more significant value because they provide access to information in formats that are not available elsewhere.

Ready access to information is very often taken for granted by those without disabilities. For example, if we need a book for a book club discussion, we have the choice of driving to a bookstore or a library to get it. If we need to do some research on the new television we want to buy, we can log on to a myriad of consumer sites or locate a consumer magazine and read about its pros and cons. For people who are blind, going to the local bookstore or library for needed titles often isn't an option because the titles are not available in a usable format. Likewise, if a person with a visual disability wants to do research on that television set, he would need to access the text with magnifying hardware or find a person willing to read the information aloud. However, if the person had access to the Internet and assistive equipment, he probably would be able to download the book title as well as reading as many reviews about the television as time permitted. Through computer access, people with disabilities can have the same opportunities as those without; however, there is a noted lag in this group to embrace the technology.

How Can Libraries Encourage People with Disabilities to Embrace Computer Technology?

A recent study conducted by the Consumer Expert Group at the request of Digital Britain determined that four issues are causing people with disabilities to not embrace the Internet.[14]

1. Lack of motivation. Persons with disabilities are often not part of the workforce and are less likely to have had to use computers. Additionally, the cost of computer technology for those in a low-income bracket is prohibitive.
2. Difficulty starting out and getting online. Often persons with disabilities lack awareness that computers can assist them. This factor is not helped by the fact that mainstream vendors

of computer equipment know little about accessibility technology and often give the wrong advice. Once the person realizes that accessible technology is available, the cost of it, coupled with training in the use of the products, makes the learning curve very steep.

3. The Internet's inaccessibility. A disconcerting fact is that many websites and applications are becoming less accessible rather than more accessible. It is disappointing for a user with a disability to learn how to use a computer, then reach sites that are inaccessible because of poor design.

4. Not fully realizing the benefits of the Internet and being afraid of Internet predators. For some people who have never used the Internet, it is hard to comprehend the vast amount of information that can be found and used, including some vital to their well-being. Also, certain groups of persons with disabilities are fearful that they may be conned online and thus avoid the Internet.

These issues can all be addressed and in part conquered with the help of the library.

Libraries can provide the technology, inform the public, make accessible sites available, and train and educate the patron. As with most educational and intellectual pursuits, libraries can make a difference in the lives of ordinary people and help them realize a potential they never knew existed.

Technology Solutions for Persons with Disabilities

It is important to remember that although the accessibility options discussed can and will be used by most persons with the disability, people and their disabilities are unique. Each person will work to find his own access solution and should never have it forced on him by an instructor. It is also important to remember that it is the library staff's job to demonstrate and educate, but not to dictate. Generally speaking, users seek solutions to make their computers easier to use, not for solutions based on their disability.[15]

Visual Impairment

The disability term *visual impairment* is a broad-based term used to describe a myriad of vision problems. Most people do have some type of impairment, whether it is being nearsighted or farsighted or having dry-eye syndrome, but they can use computers without special accommodations. However, there are also impairments that cannot be remedied, such as macular degeneration, color blindness, or simply poor vision. These people still have usable vision. For example, they may be able to drive, but they cannot read standard print (print that is smaller than 14 points; most commercial print is standard print).

People with a visual impairment will prefer using text and manipulating the text display to suit their needs. Patrons with low vision may seek to enlarge the display font just a little, or they may supersize the cursor. People who have color blindness may need to change the background on page displays. Most people with usable vision will not use a screen reader.

Blindness

The accepted definition of *legal blindness* is complicated and basically summed up as lack of the ability to see anything regardless of objects being close or far.[16] People who are blind may be able to differentiate from daylight or nighttime; however, the vision is so limited they cannot safely move about in unfamiliar areas without the aid of a cane, a guide, or a guide dog.

People who are blind need to access information aurally or by touch. People who are blind listen to books and can listen to the Internet. If they read Braille books, they can use Braille displays to access the Internet. They are best accommodated by software that reads text aloud using synthetic text-to-speech software or by using refreshable Braille displays.

Hearing Loss

The term *hearing impairment* is a general term that applies to persons who have trouble differentiating certain frequencies, localizing sounds, and hearing certain pitches. People with hearing loss are often helped with hearing aids or by seeking visual cues during conversations.[17]

Until the last few years, people with a hearing loss did not face many barriers when using the Internet and the World Wide Web. However, with the advent of product instructions being given on such sites as YouTube and the incorporation of sound clips within websites, people with a hearing loss are starting to lose the ability to fully use the Internet. People with hearing loss need visual cues and text descriptors functionality.

Deafness

Persons who are deaf lack the ability to hear any sound and are reliant on visual cues to communicate and learn. Many people who are deaf know some version of sign language (each language has its own sign language) or are proficient in lipreading. Until recently they were not hampered by too many obstacles when accessing the Internet, as it was a very visual product. Their basic need was for the computer to provide visual cues to auditory signals.

However, the Internet and the World Wide Web are becoming increasingly multisensory devices. Although visual displays are useful, unless there is text for each word spoken, some sites are not usable by people who are deaf. Using captioning and instant messaging on websites with auditory applications is necessary.

Mobility or Dexterity Issues

When speaking in relation to persons with mobility or dexterity issues, we are addressing those individuals who may need to use a wheelchair and want to slide it under a public worktable, persons who may have severe rheumatoid arthritis and cannot flex their fingers, or persons who may not be able to sit or stand for long periods of time. They may not have the ability to move their fingers across a standard keyboard or move *any* part of their limbs.

Patrons with mobility disabilities may be helped by adding different types of input devices to the library's computer tool chest. Large keyboards, small keyboards, trackballs, scanning software—the possibilities are enormous, and there is something for every need. As long as a person has control of one part of his or her body, whether the use of a finger, an eye, or a smile, they can use a computer.

Learning Disabilities

Learning disabilities are often not obvious by cursory observation, and there is no widely accepted definition of the term. People who have this disability are often bright but cannot always correctly interpret visual symbols such as letters and words as having meaning. Although some people can't read and understand text, others may not be able to see numbers correctly or perform mathematical calculations. Often, persons with learning disabilities may become easily distracted when reading and lose their thought processes. This work only seeks to address reading disabilities.

Some persons with learning disabilities succeed by hearing words as they read. For these people, there are software solutions that will help them read and learn—and enjoy the reading and learning process. HumanWare and Kurzweil Education Systems offer software that will read information aloud as words are highlighted (see appendix A for a list of vendors). If there are words that are not understood by the user, he or she may jump to a dictionary to have the word defined.

Cognitive Disabilities

Persons with cognitive disabilities generally need more time to process information, and they might be overwhelmed with the presentation of a multitude of new information. Cognitive disabilities may be congenital, may develop as a result of a physical trauma, or may be part of the aging process.

Persons with this disability might benefit from technologies such as screen readers, modifying the appearance of the screen display by eliminating ribbons or buttons, or using different types of inputting hardware. People with cognitive disabilities can learn to use computers, but it may take more time and more patience on the part of the patron with the disability and the staff trainer.

Autism and Autism Spectrum Disorders or Condition

In 1970, autism, a developmental and behavioral disorder that affects a person's verbal and nonverbal communication, understanding of language, and socialization skills, only affected 1 out of every 10,000 children.[18] Today, the Centers for Disease Control estimates that 1 out of 150 children, mostly males, have some form of autism.[19] With numbers this large, it is inevitable that people with autism or autism spectrum disorders (ASDs) or condition will be visiting the library.

Researchers, teachers, and parents of children with ASDs or condition have found that computer programs do aid their children or young adults, as computer programs are predictable and therefore controllable. They enable errors to be made safely, they offer a highly perfectible medium, and they give possibilities of nonverbal or verbal expression.[20] Computer software programs in the realm of learning basic social skills, and storyboard-writing software such as Mayer-Johnson's Boardmaker, which enables teachers to print symbols and pictures to communicate daily life needs, have been found to help individuals learn and grown intellectually and socially.

Generally speaking, people with autism are able to use a standard computer. Some, however, will need to use input devices, such as joysticks, oversize keyboards, or touch screens. Numerous software programs can teach social skills to help individuals learn how to act in social situations.

As noted earlier, some assistive technologies added to the library environment are used by people without disabilities. Similarly, some assistive technologies can be used by most people; others are used by people with specific disabilities. Table 1.1 offers a snapshot of these accessibility options with the cautionary advisement that because human beings are unique, their abilities to work with assistive technology will vary. An option may be suggested for a person who has a physical impairment only to discover the option may also help someone with a visual impairment.

What to Do First? Create an Advisory Board

It is highly unlikely that the library will have sufficient funds and staff to simultaneously install all needed technologies; thus, the accessibility initiatives will have to be done in phases. So, which do you do first, the ones that will help patrons who are blind or those who are hearing impaired? It's a tough call, but someone will have to make it.

It is suggested that the library create an advisory board made up of technology staff, a financial person, public service staff, liaisons from rehabilitation centers, and, most important, patrons with disabilities. Together, work out long- and short-term goals for the library. Before doing this, however, ask, What do we have that can improve services starting today? It may be something as simple as moving a workstation with a large monitor to a better-lit area or enabling some of Microsoft's or Apple's Macintosh accessibility attributes to be reached by creating shortcuts on the computer's desktop.

Together, staff, patrons, and professionals can access the community demographics and determine what appears to be most needed. If the library is in a community with a large amount of seniors, then tools that enlarge on-screen text would be a good place to start. If the library is in a younger community, then tools that will help students with disabilities—such as software that highlights and reads text aloud—would be a good step.

Summation: One Size Does Not Fit All

It should be noted here that although there is a vast array of both hardware and software that will help people achieve success, a device that might help one person's particular disability might create a barrier for another. Do not avoid adding technologies; just plan their placement.

Table 1.1
Accessibility Options

For Persons with:	Visual Impairments	Blindness	Learning Disabilities	Deafness	Hearing Impairments	No Disabilities	Physical / Mobility Disabilities	Autism	Cognitive Disabilities	Deaf-Blindness
Large Monitor	•		•			•	•		•	
AbleLink Web Access Suite			•					•	•	
Text Enlarging Software	•		•							
Large-Print Keytops	•		•			•			•	
Large-Print Output	•		•			•			•	•
Braille Key Tops		•								•
Raised Dot Home Keys	•		•			•				
Screen Reader / Synthesizer	•	•	•					•	•	
Braille Software Translator		•								•
Refreshable Braille Display		•								•
Braille Embosser		•								•
Speech Recognition	•	•	•				•		•	
Show Sounds				•	•	•				
Captioning Text				•	•	•				
Alternate Keyboards							•	•	•	
Trackballs							•	•	•	
Screen Display Keyboards							•			
Text Browser Software	•	•						•	•	
Headphones	•	•	•		•	•		•	•	
OCR Scanning	•	•	•					•	•	
Correctly Designed Websites	•	•	•	•	•	•	•	•	•	•
Touch Screen			•			•		•	•	
Storyboards								•		
Jelly Bean Switch								•	•	
Nontraditional mice	•						•	•	•	
Zac Browser								•		
Videophone				•	•					
Skype Video Call				•	•					
Sorenson Video Relay				•	•					
IntelliKeys							•	•	•	
Adjustable Work-table	•	•	•	•	•	•	•	•	•	•

It is important to remember the obvious, that people with disabilities are individuals. Their personalities, values, intellectual abilities, and social mores will all affect their willingness and ability to learn computer skills with assistive devices. More than likely, the library will not be able to have all solutions for all people with disabilities, but having solutions for most people with disabilities is acceptable.

Notes

1. American Foundation for the Blind, "Special Report on Aging and Vision Loss," September 2008, www.afb.org/Section.asp?SectionID=15& DocumentID=4423.
2. World Health Organization, "Global Burden of Disease. Part 3: Disease Incidence, Prevalence and Disability," www.who.int/healthinfo/global _burden_disease/GBD_report_2004update_part3.pdf.
3. The U.S. Census Bureau, American FactFinder, 2005–2007, http:// factfinder.census.gov/servlet/STTable?_bm=y&-qr_name=ACS_2007_3YR _G00_S1801&-geo_id=01000US&-ds_name=ACS_2007_3YR_G00_.
4. Ibid.
5. Ibid.
6. The American Foundation for the Blind maintains a user-friendly database, AFB's Statistical Snapshots, at www.afb.org/Section.asp?SectionID=15, which provides facts and figures on people with vision loss.
7. The Americans with Disabilities Act (ADA) is civil rights legislation extending the protection of the law and guaranteeing equal access to employment, public services and accommodations, transportation, and telecommunications to people with disabilities. For more information, visit the Americans with Disabilities website, www.ada.gov. Section 504, part of the Rehabilitation Act, forbids individuals with disabilities from being excluded from services or programs. To read more about the legislation, see www.hhs.gov/ocr/civilrights/resources/factsheets/504.pdf. Section 508 of the Rehabilitation Act requires federal agencies to make their electronic and information technology accessible to people with disabilities. The agency retains an information-rich website at www.section508.gov/index.cfm? FuseAction=Content&ID=3.
8. American Library Association, "Access to Library Resources Regardless of Sex, Gender, Identity, Gender Expression, or Sexual Orientation," Interpretation of the American Library Association Library Bill of Rights, Amended July 2, 2008, www.ala.org/ala/aboutala/offices/oif/statementspols/ statementsif/interpretations/Access%20to%20Library%20Re.pdf.

9. American Library Association, "Service to Persons with Disabilities, an Interpretation of the Library Bill of Rights," January 2009, www.ala.org/ala/aboutala/offices/oif/statementspols/statementsif/interpretations/servicespeopledisabilities.cfm.

10. The Center for Universal Design, "About UD," www.design.ncsu.edu/cud/about_ud/about_ud.htm. Further information about universal design can be found at CAST, http://cast.org, and the Institute for Human Centered Design, www.humancentereddesign.org.

11. Ibid.

12. Web Accessibility Initiative (WAI), "Introduction to Web Accessibility," "What Is Web Accessibility?" www.w3.org/WAI/intro/accessibility.php.

13. Microsoft Corporation, "Accessible Technology in Computing—Examining Awareness, Use, and Future Potential," http://microsoft.com/enable/research/phase2.aspx?v=p.

14. The Government Monitor, "Digital Britain: Barriers and Solutions to Internet Use by Persons with Disabilities," October 15, 2009, http://thegovmonitor .com/world_news/britain/digital-britain-barriers-and-solutions-to-internet -use-by-persons-with-disabilities-12098.html.

15. Microsoft, "Accessible Technology."

16. A technical definition of *legal blindness* may be found at www.articlesbase .com/vision-articles/definition-of-legal-blindness-1427410.html. The definition is based on tenets established in 1931 by the American Medical Association.

17. A technical definition of *hearing loss* may be found at www.answers.com/topic/hearing-impairment-1.

18. Autism Key, "All about Autism and Autism Spectrum Disorders," www .autismkey.com/what_is_autism.htm.

19. Ibid.

20. National Autistic Society, "Computers: Applications for People with Autism," www.nas.org.uk/nas/jsp/polopoly.jsp?d=108&a=3276. There is a multitude of resources concerning computers in relation to persons with autism on this site.

2
Creating Accessible Electronic Information

Contributed by William R. Reed IV

Every minute of every day useful (as well as ephemeral) information is being made available to the public via the Internet. Some of this information is found on websites, some in electronic databases, and still others in personal blogs. However, if the information is not presented in a usable and accessible format, it does not have value to all users.

When information providers start to think about the process of placing information in the public arena, usability and accessibility should always be first and foremost in their minds. Regardless of how unique and how valuable the information is, if it is not presented in a usable and accessible format, it will not be information that seekers will want to use and will not be information that people using assistive technology will be able to find.

Web Pages

Creating web pages that are accessible is not difficult, nor does it have to cost more to accomplish. It does, however, take commitment and adherence to accessibility guidelines. It takes resolve not to incorporate the latest electronic applications just because they are available, as they may be inaccessible to some computer users. Libraries should never create barriers around their virtual libraries, and they should encourage vendors of electronic media to have electronic collections that are usable by all their patrons.

The first step to designing an accessible web page is to know what defines a page as being accessible. Essentially, a web page that is accessible gives people with disabilities the ability to independently access and use the information that is comparable to the way people without a disability access and use the information.

Although the task of creating a website that is accessible to a cross section of society that has various disabilities seems impossible, start by looking at the population as the World Wide Web Consortium (W3C) and the U.S. Access Board responsible for Section 508 of the Rehabilitation Act did. Both of these groups have published detailed web-design guidelines based on the following concepts:[1]

- People with disabilities gain access to the Internet using a variety of adaptive hardware and software.
- Some people may not have the ability to hear, move, see, speak, or effectively comprehend or process information or text.
- Some people may not have the means to operate a keyboard or pointing device.

These factors should always be kept in mind when the library's web pages are developed and maintained.[2]

Think Accessible as You Create

Although creating accessible web pages may appear to be difficult, it is not. Authoritative standards for evaluating electronic resources and information technology are already available from the World Wide Web Consortium's Web Accessibility Initiative (WAI), Section 508 of the Rehabilitation Act, and the U.S. Access Board. Because the standards might be more than library staffs have time to assimilate, a group of the American Library Association's Association for Specialized and Cooperative Library Agencies (ASCLA) members sifted through the aforementioned guidelines and produced a tool entitled "Internet and Web-Based Content Accessibility Checklist."[3] The following is an abridgement of the tool kit.[4]

1. **If using graphical images on a page, did the designer include a meaningful text equivalent?** Words need to be added to describe what an item actually is, why it is there, and any information being communicated by the use of that item or the item itself. This includes items such as images, graphics, audio clips, applets, tickers, or other features that convey meaning through a picture or sound. It is very important to adaptive technology users that all images have accurate and meaningful text equivalents. It is also acceptable to simply include a text description next to, above, or below the image. For example, begin "The picture directly below shows . . ." Any audio should have a text equivalent, such as a text transcript.

2. **The use of multimedia should not be critical to the understanding of the information displayed.** An easy way to determine if the website works is to turn off the sound and view the presentation; can you navigate the content without sound? Then turn the monitor off and listen to the sound; does it make sense? Audio description needs to be added to the application for those who cannot see and captioning for those who cannot hear, and they need to work in tandem. An audio webcast would require a text equivalent. A silent web slide show, however, would only require a text equivalent for images used. Low-cost captioning software is available; however, audio description for video displays requires human intervention.[5]

3. **If color was removed, would it inhibit use of the website?** An easy way to check how coloring affects a web page is to view the page in high contrast (black on white, white on black, etc.) or print a page to a black-and-white printer. Examine the page and judge whether users still use the page effectively when color has been removed. Also, examine if color is being used to emphasize text or indicate an action. If so, an alternate method needs to be included so users can identify what is being emphasized or indicated. For example, if users are prompted to press a green start button,

then a text label above the green button saying "Press the green start button below" is an acceptable method.

4. **Do web pages ignore user-defined style sheets?** Style sheets are formatting instructions on how a page should be displayed. Users should be able to specify their own settings. To check, disable style sheets within the browser (consult the browser's help menu for instructions) or try changing the font size or background colors through the browser's settings.

5. **If a link is embedded in an image, is there an equivalent text link?** Frequently, web designers will use an image map that contains a link or set of links to the web page or site. Check to see if the image has any text links or labels. These text labels alert users that by clicking or selecting the link in this particular region of the image, it will retrieve a specific web page. This is an example of a client-side image map. These can be quite accommodating to people with disabilities and those using adaptive technology. Refrain from using server-side image maps that do not indicate to the user which specific web page will be retrieved when a particular region of the image is selected.

6. **If information is displayed using a table, can columns and rows be identified by screen readers?** An easy-to-check method is to use a screen reader and listen to how the table is read aloud. Any table used should include a title; moreover, all the appropriate columns and rows should also include titles that clearly identify the data set. While listening, also determine whether the information has been presented in a logical order.

7. **If frames are used, are they accurately text labeled?** Frames are used to visually separate information on a web page. Check that the frames have appropriate text labels identifying the information contained inside them. Also, test to see if you can easily move between frames using the keyboard.

8. **Does anything on the page blink or flicker?** Blinking or flashing elements should avoid frequencies between 2 Hz and 55 Hz. This requirement is necessary because some

individuals with photosensitive epilepsy can have a seizure triggered by displays that flicker or flash, particularly if the flash has a high intensity and is within this frequency range. Some users with autism are also negatively affected by blinking or flashing elements.

9. **Do websites not conforming to acceptable and approved accessibility standards offer a text-only equivalent of their website?** Each page of the website should have a text-only page. The text-only link should be easy to find and be concurrent with the non-text-only page.

10. **If scripting is used (such as Java, etc.), is there a text equivalent so adaptive technology, like screen readers, can read the information?** Scripting (such as a stock ticker) on a web page that is animated, constantly refreshing, and displaying information should have an accurate text equivalent. If it does not, it is important that users can easily disable scripting that does not affect the use of the web page.

11. **If a page uses a special applet, plug-in, or application to view information, is there a link on the same page for users to download the utility they need to access and display the information?** The applet, plug-in, application, or method(s) for displaying the information should be accessible or compatible with adaptive technology (or both) and be fairly easy to download or install.

12. **If online forms are used, can people using adaptive technology fill in and submit all the required information?** Patrons should be able to use a keyboard (as opposed to a mouse) to access all the form fields on a web page. Text labels should be used either inside or near form fields to identify what information users should be entering. Verify that a screen reader can identify the form(s) and whether they follow a logical order. For example, if users hear "last name," is the corresponding form the area where they would enter their last names?

13. **Is there a way for users, especially those using screen readers, to skip repetitive navigational links?** Navigational links are used to move visitors to pages within a website. They

are usually located on the top or side of each web page. For example, "Help" and "Contact Us" links will appear on the same page within a website in exactly the same way and location. It is useful to include a link (could be visible to screen readers only) before the navigational links that reads "Skip navigation" or "Jump to main content"; otherwise, the screen reader will read all the links all the time.

14. **If users are given a certain amount of time for an action or response, is there an indication of how much time they have left or an option to request more time?** Some web pages may expire or time-out after a certain amount of time and refresh the entire page. Be aware some users may need more time. The web pages should be dynamic enough to allow the user to request additional time if needed.

15. **Is there a help page or easily identifiable contact for users who need further assistance?** The website should offer patrons a useful, accessible help page and include any special instructions for those using adaptive technologies. Some websites may provide a navigation guide that describes the design or layout of the website or web page. Patrons should always have the option to contact by phone, instant messaging, or e-mail for technical support.

Presenting Web Page Content to the User

Some web visitors may have a disability that prevents them from easily assimilating information. They must have information presented clearly to follow directions. For the most part, websites generally fall under two styles with respect to how they present their content to a user. Both take about the same amount of time to design and mount, yet they are not equally as accessible.

The first style is a descriptive approach. Language and text on the page actually lead the user through a page or site. For example, consider a library that offers access to its online public-access catalog through its website. By adding a descriptive phrase, such as "Type the author, title, subject, or any keywords in the text box provided below, then hit Enter on the keyboard or click on the Search button to begin your search," the library has given visitors all the information they need to conduct a search. Some people might not realize that they need to notify the search engine to begin.

The second style could be called the "Here it is" approach. Everything a site has to offer is posted on the home page, and the users have to browse through a gauntlet of links and announcements to search the site for the information they want. Unfortunately, people using screen readers have the hardest time with these types of sites because a multitude of links begin to ramble at them once they download a page, and they can easily become overwhelmed and disorientated.

The "Here it is" type of presentation is best suited for people who have the ability to point-and-click throughout a page and can visually sort through the content of a website. This style often frustrates people using screen readers, unless they have become so familiar with a particular site that they can immediately go to the pages they want. By using descriptive language and styles, Web developers can help prevent their easily accessible sites from becoming incomprehensible.

Does This Website Really Work?

The best way to understand the importance of providing accessible web pages is to view web pages with a multisensory approach (i.e., listen to them, read them, and try to operate them as someone using adaptive technologies would). Web page designers should consider the following points of view:

- What if you had to wait to hear the screen reader read the entire page to find the text-only link?
- What if you had to "click here" and could not see where to "click here"?
- How aggravating would it be to have an assortment of colors flashing and banners refreshing while trying to use screen magnification software?
- How distracting are altering background and text colors, multimedia, applets, and Java scripting to people with attention disorders or learning disabilities?
- Would you have the patience to browse through or listen to twenty, thirty, or fifty links before finding what you wanted?

These represent only some of the access issues encountered by people who are disabled and trying to use the Internet. Website developers really haven't experienced the Internet from the point of view of a person with disabilities until they have tried to navigate the Internet using adaptive technologies such as Braille displays, screen readers and magnifiers, learning-systems software for those with learning disabilities, natural language technologies, on-screen keyboards, switches (devices used by people with severe disabilities that emulate actions performed by the keyboard or mouse and are tailored to the individual's strengths), and other mouse or keyboard emulators. Essentially, people with disabilities have been given this wonderful and limitless resource and been told to find a way to use it themselves.

Thanks to organizations such as the Access Board of the World Wide Web Consortium and the Section 508 Access Board, steps are being taken to ensure web developers have the blueprints and methodology for constructing accessible sites. More websites are adhering to the guidelines or have gone beyond them, offering audio output or ways of enlarging users' displays through their site rather than relying on text-to-speech engines or screen magnification software.[6]

Have "Others" Test the Web Pages for Accessibility

Testing of web content by accessibility specialists and by users using assistive technology is a necessary part of any significant web-development effort. It is suggested that the library simply ask users of assistive technology to try the website that is said to be found accessible before it is launched. If this is not possible, web-based evaluators are available. Although these evaluation tools may not ensure 100 percent compliance, they will ensure the website has an acceptable compliance.[7] The following two products are useful and available without cost:

> NCAM Web Accessibility QA Favelet. Available from the National Center for Accessible Media (NCAM), the Web Accessibility QA Favelet will help staff through a structured Q&A process to identify accessibility issues on web pages. The product works with browsers such as Internet Explorer and Firefox and works within the Windows and MAC environments.[8]
>
> WAVE (Web Accessibility Evaluation Tool). A product of WebAIM, WAVE takes people through the web accessibility evaluation process either through entering page URLs within the WebAIM site or by downloading the WAVE toolbar, which works with the Firefox browser.[9] WAVE keeps it simple

by displaying the original web page with embedded icons and indicators that reveal the accessibility of that page. The WAVE Firefox toolbar enables evaluation directly through the browser, allowing the evaluation of password-protected, secure, or otherwise sensitive web content. Because the evaluation is done within the browser, dynamically created, modified, or scripted content can be evaluated in real time. The product is free, and it also has a Spanish-language option.

Making a website accessible does not necessarily mean making it boring or plain. Attracting visitors is the main goal of a web designer, and by following these principles along with employing some creativity, a universally accessible web presence can be constructed offering the greatest accessibility to all visitors.

Electronic Databases and Computer Software

Electronic databases and computer software also fall under the category of electronic and information technology. Similar to Internet web pages, these resources need to be evaluated for accessibility. The good news is that many of the same accessibility checkpoints used for web pages also apply to computer software and electronic databases. So, library staff will not have to learn a whole new set of criteria checkpoints; they can just modify their approach using the following considerations when evaluating the accessibility of these items.

Vendors should be made to comply with the library's accessibility goals. Those that do not should be put on notice that compliance is necessary. The more libraries that put database vendors on notice, the greater the chance for remedying access issues.

Twelve Yes Answers Required

Often the task of purchasing databases is left to staff members who are seeking specific outcomes for their specialty areas. When they find products, they are elated and do not ask if patrons using assistive technologies can also use them as well. A set of questions were developed by an ad hoc group of librarians, from libraries for the blind, university libraries, public libraries, and state libraries, many of whom experienced the frustration of not being able to use all databases because of accessibility issues. The librarians represented a good cross section of the country and included a librarian who worked abroad. The questions were crafted to elicit only a yes as an acceptable response. Acquisition librarians for electronic databases are encouraged to print the questions and use them for the products they purchase to enable them to "buy accessible."[10]

Listed below are those questions with explanations of their purpose.

1. **Can just a keyboard be used to effectively operate this software?** This is perhaps the most important and often neglected consideration. All tasks should be able to be accomplished through the keyboard and not be mouse dependent.

2. **Can you use the software while running adaptive technology or basic operating system accessibility options?** Can the software be used with basic operating system accessibility options (Windows or Mac), such as FilterKeys, Screen Magnifiers, Narrators, On-Screen Keyboards, Sticky Keys, visual warnings such as SoundSentry when sounds are made, and so forth? Can assistive technology work effectively and in harmony with the software? If the software disables or ignores any of the assistive technology or user-enabled accessibility options, it is not a product that all can use.

3. **Does the software have any of its own accessibility features to assist users?** The software should have user-enabled accessibility options, such as changing font size or background color, and so forth, that actually assist the user.

4. **If using assistive technology, can users distinguish where they are on the display?** When screens change or new windows open or close, headings or titles should be available to help users identify where they are and perhaps what to do next. Also, check if a screen reader correctly identifies the focus (currently active item, screen, or window). It is very easy for screen reader users to get lost when multiple windows start opening on their screens; therefore, the software should enable users to determine which window is active.

5. **Have controls and functions for operating the software been properly labeled or described?** Verify that buttons, check

boxes, menus, toolbars, images, form fields, and any user-action function of the software have a text-label description that correctly describes the action. For example, if a user's focus is on the Search button, does the screen reader say "Search button"?

6. **Are images associated with certain user actions consistent and labeled throughout the program?** User actions, such as printing, saving, searching, and so forth, that are associated with an icon or image should be used in the same way throughout the product. For example, if an image of a printer is clicked to send a document to the printer, ensure that an alternate text tag appears identifying the image and that this tag is consistent throughout the software.

7. **Can all text be read when using adaptive technology, especially screen magnifiers and readers?** Does the software run through the operating system's window, or does it run through its own window? For example, Microsoft Word runs through a Windows operating system window, and Windows is controlling how text is displayed on the screen. Some products run through their own windows and control how text is displayed, not the operating system. These products have a greater chance of not being accessible to adaptive technology. Check that all the text that is displayed and entered into form fields can be read with screen magnifiers, readers, and other voice-output adaptive technologies

8. **If used, can any animation be disabled? Is there a text equivalent for any information displayed using animation?** There should be user controls for disabling and enabling animations through the keyboard. Also, evaluate if screen readers or other adaptive technology can correctly read or identify the animation. If the animation cannot be disabled, does it allow assistive technology to perform its assigned tasks? A text script of the animation should be available.

9. **If color were removed, would the operating software still be functional?** If the display was viewed from a monochrome (white on black, green on black, etc.) monitor or printed from

a black-and-white printer, could users still effectively distinguish visual elements? Reference to color should not be the sole directive on pages.

10. **If users can adjust screen colors, do the color choices allow for a variety of contrasts?** Does the program allow users to change the background color, font color, contrast, and so forth, and does it offer a variety of basic and custom colors? Software should offer options to choose preset high and low contrast and soft background settings.

11. **If there are elements of the display that blink or flash, can they be disabled?** Vendors should demonstrate that any blinking or flashing elements have a blink or flash frequency lower than 2 Hz or greater than 55 Hz. This requirement is necessary because some individuals with photosensitive epilepsy can have a seizure triggered by displays that flicker or flash, particularly if the flash has a high intensity and is within a certain frequency range. Additionally, blinking and flashing may cause problems for users with autism spectrum disorders.

12. **Can adaptive technology users effectively enter information where appropriate?** Users should have access to all form fields solely through the keyboard. Forms should have descriptive text labels inside the form fields as this enables users to know what information should be typed into each form field.

Don't Be Exclusionary

Good intentions will not solve access problems. Adhering to accessibility guidelines, resisting temptations to use web applications simply because they are popular, and advocacy are ways for change. It may be uncomfortable to tell a vendor that the library will not purchase a database unless it can be used by all the library's patrons, but this is how change is accomplished. Likewise, seeking the advice of professionals who monitor electronic information is useful. They know the problems; they know the success stories as well.[11]

Notes

1. The Section 508 guidelines and the W3C guidelines may be viewed in their entirety at www.Section508.gov and www.w3.org/standards/, respectively.
2. "Web Design and Accessibility through a Trainer's Eyes and Accessibility beyond Equipment and Web Design," *Library Technology Reports* 37, no. 4 (July/August 2001): 45–46.
3. The task force consisted of librarians who assisted patrons with disabilities as well as librarians who use assistive technology for their own access needs. To see ALA's ASCLA "Internet and Web-Based Content Checklist" in its entirety, visit www.ala.org/ala/mgrps/divs/ascla/asclaprotools/thinkaccessible/internetwebguidelines.cfm.
4. The Section 508 guidelines and the W3C guidelines may be viewed in their entirety at www.Section508.gov and www.w3.org/standards/, respectively.
5. California State University Northridge, Accessibility Technology Initiative, "Ten Checkpoints for Accessibility," www.csun.edu/accessibility/checkpoints .html. To view properly presented video web content, visit "Introduction to Screen Readers," at www.doit.wisc.edu/accessibility/video/intro.asp.
6. "Web Design and Accessibility through a Trainer's Eyes," 60–64.
7. A complete list of website evaluation tools may be found on the W3C website, www.w3.org/WAI/RC/tools/complete/. Some of these products will identify specific site problems and offer solutions.
8. The NCAM Web Accessibility QA Favelet can be downloaded at http://ncam .wgbh.org/invent_build/web_multimedia/tools-guidelines/favelet/.
9. WAVE can be downloaded from WebAIM's website, http://wave.webaim.org.
10. ALA, ASCLA, Accessibility for Electronic Media, "Think Accessible before You Buy: Questions to Ask to Ensure That the Electronic Resources Your Library Plans to Purchase Are Accessible," www.ala.org/ala/mgrps/divs/ascla/asclaprotools/thinkaccessible/default.cfm.
11. Axel Schmetzke, "Web Accessibility Survey," http://library.uwsp.edu/aschmetz/Accessible/websurveys.htm. In addition to providing accessibility overviews of electronic products vendors both in the United States and abroad, Schmetzke offers links to a myriad of topics concerning web access. Additionally, the website offers an example of a well-designed website in regard to access.

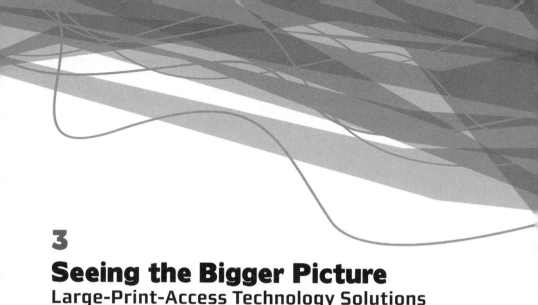

3
Seeing the Bigger Picture
Large-Print-Access Technology Solutions

Although some people are born with visual impairments, others become visually impaired later in their life span. Diseases such as macular degeneration and uncontrolled diabetes can cause one's vision to worsen during life. A study commissioned by Microsoft determined that the average age of the computer user is increasing and that in ten years, there will be 2.5 times as many adults who range in age from sixty-five to seventy-four using computers as there are today.[1] It is acknowledged that aging does bring about disabilities that affect one's ability to use technology, meaning the total number of people with difficulties and impairments and needing assistive technology will increase.[2]

People who have some usable vision or who lose their vision later in life will prefer to use large print, as it is familiar. There are actually many options to do this, and at least one is more than likely already available on computers owned by the library. These are accessibility options provided with most Microsoft and Apple operating systems.

Large-print access is not only an accommodation for persons with vision loss. Persons with some types of learning disabilities find accessing large-print displays vital to the learning process.[3] Additionally, some computer users with cognitive disabilities find information displayed in large print easier to absorb.

Providing large-print-access is perhaps the easiest accommodation to execute. Embracing the concept of universal design, staff can actually establish a large-print-access station for general use. Few patrons are hindered by large-print accommodations.

Lighting and Location

Good lighting in the area where assistive devices are installed is essential. As we age, the need for additional light increases. By the time we are fifty, we will need twice as much light as we did when we were twenty-five. Thus, it is important to provide good overhead light as well as task lighting.[4]

A good task lamp or magnifying task lamp works in conjunction with the patron's usable vision, ambient lighting, and the enlarging device to optimize the output of the technology. It is a disservice to place workstations in low-lit areas without providing a way for the patron to read printed instructions and see the keyboard. Fluorescent lighting is a good choice as it is low cost and mimics natural light. These lamps can be found in hobby stores as well as through low-vision specialty suppliers.

It is important to place the workstation designed for patrons with low vision in an accessible area of the library where the user can enjoy maximum safety by librarians ensuring book trucks, stools, and crawling children are not a part of the pathway. The area should be free from glare and shadows. When placing the equipment, seek to protect the privacy of the patron using the equipment as well as that of the library's other customers, as text and graphics displayed on the oversize monitor have a way of catching the attention of people just passing by. The library would not want to create embarrassing situations for either.

Graphics and buildings staff should ensure that signage used directing patrons to the workstation and all documents expected to be used by the patron in the workstation are done in a format that is usable by the patron. Lettering used in signage should be sans serif. Block lettering is easiest to discern by people with low vision and by those with a reading disability that makes it difficult for them to see words. Good signs will also aid persons with hearing impairments, as well as learning differences, as they are essential to independent pathfinding. When selecting a font, ask a staff member who has low vision if he or she can read the letters and numbers correctly. Some fonts are just easier to read by people with low vision. Figure 3.1 gives an idea of font legibility.

Figure 3.1
Legibility of 12-Point Fonts

Click here	Bookman Old Style
Click here	*Mistral*
Click here	Arial
Click here	Courier New
Click here	Occidental
Click here	Times New Roman
Click here	Tahoma
Click here	Comic Sans MS

Although all of the fonts in this display are 12 point, note that some are easier to read.

Monitors and Keyboards

One of the first items to add in regard to large-print access is an oversize flat-screen monitor; nineteen inches or larger is recommended. It does little good to magnify words on smaller screens because continuity is lost as letters become larger and larger. It is markedly more helpful to see an entire word or phrase than one or two letters, which happens when using large-print software on a standard monitor.

It is also helpful to provide keyboards that have large typefaces for those users who do not have touch-typing skills or are unfamiliar with the keyboard. There are two ways to accomplish this. One way is to purchase a large-print keyboard (as shown in figure 3.2); the other is to purchase pres-ply large-print key tops and convert a standard keyboard to a large-print keyboard. Pres-ply large-print key tops come on a sheet and are simply peeled off the sheet and applied to the keyboard. All the letters and functions are included. These items are available from distributors of low-vision products, some of which are listed in appendix A.

Software

Microsoft Products

Microsoft has included some type of accessibility feature with its operating systems since DOS and has sought to improve or expand on them with each

Figure 3.2
Large-Print Keyboard

This large-print keyboard provides computer users who are unfamiliar with the keyboard a clearer view of the keys.

release of the Windows product. Locating and accessing these utilities is dependent on the version of Windows used; however, later versions of Windows established an Access Center, which is implemented through the Control Panel.[5]

Although the accessibility features that come with Windows are not as advanced as those of specialized products, they can be activated without delay and will help some of the library's patrons immediately. Information technology staff members are encouraged to develop a procedure that will allow staff who are assisting patrons using computers to turn the features on. If security is an issue, at the very least designate a few of the library's computers for large-print displays and use the largest font possible. Set it as the default.

Included within Microsoft Windows Accessibility features suite are functions that offer the patron several options:

- The user can adjust the display options by enlarging the font size; later editions allow up to sixteen times (16x) magnification.
- The user can change the size and color of the icons, making them easier to see.
- The user can adjust the screen resolution and develop personalized high-contrast schemes that are easier to see.

- For patrons with really low vision, it will allow a narrator feature to be activated that reads text on the screen aloud and describes some events (such as an error message appearing) that happen while using the computer. It is not as sophisticated as software designed for this purpose.

The Windows 7's Magnifier is being praised by many low-vision users who cannot afford to purchase the professionally designed products. Users feel that this is a viable option for screen enlargement. The keyboard short-cuts and magnifying options are usable and valuable, while the magnifier feature helps the user to find buttons. The keyboard shortcut features can also be useful for people with learning disabilities who need to cut through the clutter.

Apple Products

Apple's Mac OS-X has quite a few products that enable patrons with some types of visual disabilities to have access to information. It is not obvious, however, that these products will work within the environment of special-ized software products. The Apple accessibility products are found on the Universal Access Panel and are actually quite detailed. The following products are available:

- Zoom, a built-in, full-screen magnifier that can magnify the items on the screen up to forty times (40x)
- Cursor magnification, which can be used independently or in conjunction with Zoom
- High-contrast and reverse-video features, which allow the user to adjust the display to a black-and-white display or reverse the colors so that black images are white and the background is black
- Dock magnification, which enables the user to point to and enlarge all icons, applications, files, and folders parked in the docking area
- Talking alerts, which voice aloud messages deemed important to the user
- Icon view and Cover view, which enable the user to preview folder contents in a larger display

Keyboard shortcuts are also part of Apple's accessibility package and enable users to quickly jump to the utility they need. Shortcut icons on the desktop alert patrons with some vision, as well as those with learning or cognitive disabilities, that assistance is available.

Specialized Screen Enlargers

Screen-magnifying software programs were originally developed for people with low vision, and such programs primarily are still the preferred magnifying choice. Screen magnifiers can magnify the contents displayed on the computer screen from two to thirty-six times (2x to 36x). In addition to magnifying text and cursors, screen-magnification programs allow the user to change the way the text looks, the display colors, and the background colors. The screen-enlarging limits are the physical size of the computer screen itself and the user's ability to retain fragments of words and thoughts he or she reads on the screen. Aware of the limitation of the screen, some new applications of professional text magnifiers allow the user to use two monitors side by side to read the text, which allows him or her to enlarge the text to the maximum, as the viewing area has been doubled.

Screen-enlarging packages are not inexpensive, and the one the library chooses should be one that is used by patrons who live within the library's service area. A query to local vendors as well as to persons with low vision, or schools that have students with learning disabilities and use a screen enlarger, will enable the library to select a package with confidence.

ZoomText

ZoomText was created by the Ai Squared company, whose mission is to provide large-print access to electronic text, and it is one of the very first products of this type developed. ZoomText enables the user to clearly, and without distortion, magnify text up to thirty-six times (36x) by using a mouse or keyboard commands. It allows the user to use web applications as well as word-processing applications by providing easy-to-use search windows. The software is flexible and allows the user to change the pointer display, enhance the color contrasts of displays, and change color displays. ZoomText also has focus enhancements that act as a handheld magnifier by moving over certain areas of the screen, enlarging just that part. The text display from ZoomText is always clear and undistorted, even when taken to the maximum magnification, as the program fills in missing parts of the letters as they get stretched to larger sizes.

ZoomText now has a feature that will allow the user to see text on two monitors as if there was an extra-large, oversize monitor. What this does is allow the user to have more thought continuity. Doubling the amount of words the user can see helps with the reading process and the ability to assimilate information. Figure 3.3 shows a typical enlargement display using the ZoomText software.

One version of ZoomText, the ZoomText Magnifier Reader, lends audio output to what is being displayed on-screen. The program narrates all actions

Figure 3.3
ZoomText Display

Using this commercial screen-enlarging software, persons with low vision are able to magnify text and graphics, enabling them to see the display.

but can be adjusted to only speak what the user needs spoken. For example, the software can be programmed to only read apps, or it can be programmed to echo what is being typed. This is great for the user who is unsure of his or her typing ability. The product does not interfere with screen-reading software such as JAWS (for more on JAWS, see chapter 4).

A relatively new product that is also useful for users who are unsure of their typing ability is the ZoomText Large Print Keyboard. Although the keyboard has easy-to-see, large-print key tops, a greater attribute is the eighteen added function buttons, which give users the ability to jump straight to the feature of ZoomText they need to use. If the library is choosing ZoomText for a workstation that will be used by persons with low vision or a learning disability, consider purchasing the keyboard. The library would have a sturdy keyboard with large-print key displays and the shortcut keys, which can shorten the learning curve for new users.

ZoomText is also available on a USB drive (as shown in figure 3.4) and allows the installation and use of ZoomText whenever and wherever needed without having to purchase additional licensing or activation. Once Zoom-Text has been installed on a system, ZoomText will automatically start up and be ready to use each time you plug in the USB drive. This may be useful on computers that have a lot of programs on them, as this program will immediately start when plugged into a computer.

Figure 3.4
ZoomText on USB

Many of today's screen-enlarging software programs are formatted for USB drives, which enables the software to travel with the user.

The learning curve for staff and patrons is a small one. The company supports excellent, easy-to-use online tutorials and webinars.[6]

MAGic for Windows

MAGic for Windows is a screen-magnifier product of Freedom Scientific from its broad-based product line that provides options for users with a variety of needs. The MAGic screen magnifier allows the user to customize the way in which information is displayed by allowing a tint to be added to the screen or by making the screen appear to be monochrome. Users can also switch brightness as well as the colors of the text or the background. Screen glare, a culprit that causes low-vision users much difficulty, is eliminated by having the ability to boost the contrast. It is also possible to keep track of your pointer by adjusting the controls. Speech output comes with MAGic, which assists users in navigation through documents.

The strongest selling point of MAGic for many institutions is that it comes from the company that produces the screen reader JAWS for Windows. As a result, there is full compatibility with the product, and some of the keystroke commands are the same; plus, the library will be dealing with one company rather than two.

The learning curve for staff and patrons is a small one, as commands are logical and easy to access. The product comes with five hours' worth of built-in training tools.[7]

Lunar, LunarPlus, and SuperNova

The Lunar and LunarPlus (with speech prompts) software programs from Dolphin Computer Access, a United Kingdom company, offer many of the same features as their product peers. These software products enable readers to increase and manipulate information displayed on the monitor, such as the ability to enlarge the pointer and the ability to magnify user-defined areas of the monitor.

The Lunar line offers some unique features, such as Margin Release, which adds some extra blank space around the edges of the screen. As the user approaches the edges of the real screen, the mouse remains in the central area of the monitor. This helps users with poor peripheral vision, as the strong change in contrast is a clear indicator that they are approaching the edge of the real screen. Additionally, there are twenty-three predetermined popular color-combination views users can choose from besides allowing them to find their own. This is good for the novice user who is not yet tech-nologically savvy.

SuperNova is a unique product that offers the standard screen magnifier but also offers a full screen reader and Braille support. With few exceptions, it is unlikely that a Braille user will also use a large-print display (an exception being teachers of both people who are visually impaired or blind). This is good for a public-access venue that may have a variety of users.

Although Dolphin Computer Access supports a wide variety of tutorials, it is a United Kingdom–based company, and local support in the United States may be problematic if the software is not used in the library's area.[8] However, new distributors are being added. If Dolphin is popular in your area, it is a viable option.[9]

WinZoom and WinZoom USB

Clarity Technology, which makes and supports portable magnification prod-ucts and the screen magnifier WinZoom, also manufactures WinZoom USB, a low-cost product that can be used with any Windows-compatible computer. Staff or the patron can simply plug it in, and the autoplay feature will be launched. One does not have to install any software or drivers, meaning once it is unplugged, there is no trace of the device having been there. It is compatible with XP and Vista, will magnify from 1.5 to 36 points, has a smoothing feature, and offers a voice assist.

WinZoom also allows the user to change color displays, align text to max-imize the vision the user has, enlarge the mouse pointer or other locators, and add tracking to let the user know where he or she is in the document. There are also such features as typing echo and mouse echo, which let users hear what they are inputting and some narration. The program comes pre-loaded on a memory stick. Should the library be interested in this product, the company offers a free trial of the product.[10]

Virtual Magnifying Glass

Virtual Magnifying Glass offers an alternative for those without a budget and whose needs are not met by Microsoft's utilities. Virtual Magnifying Glass is a free, open-source, cross-platform screen-magnification tool. It does demand information technology (IT) knowledge to get it installed and working. The library's staff need either to be able to use Lazarus, an open-source RAD IDE, or Borland Delphi, as well as having some knowledge of Pascal and a little

Delphi VCL.[11] Once it is installed, it does provide magnification options and logical shortcut key options similar to those of the commercial packages, but it does not come with support. On a positive note, most consumers who have downloaded the free product find it easy to use.

Hardware

CCTV

Perhaps the greatest advance that has been made in the area of hardware for persons with low vision has been that of closed-circuit televisions (CCTVs). The concept of a CCTV is a simple one to understand. A video camera is used in real time to capture the image of the reading materials (this could be newspapers, personal correspondence, pictures, etc.) or objects placed

Figure 3.5
CCTV Use

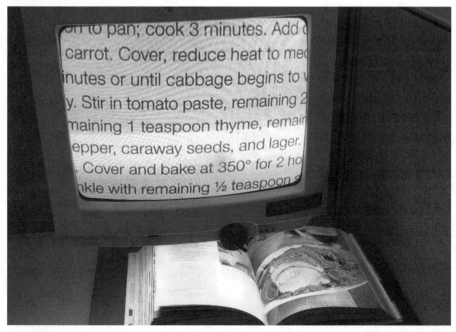

Although an older technology, CCTV provides persons with low vision a magnified look at an infinite variety of print materials, photographs, and three-dimensional objects.

in the viewing area and display the image on a monitor in a larger size or in a different color contrast. (Figure 3.5 shows a typical CCTV setup.) It is a very simple-to-use device with a very small learning curve. Most tabletop CCTVs will enlarge items from two and one-half times (2.5x) to seventy-two times (72x) the actual size.

CCTVs are still a well-respected and much-used option for libraries and should be available for use in all libraries. The model the library selects should be based on budget, ease of use, and the availability of local support. It is helpful to talk to a distributor of a wide range of CCTVs to discuss options as opposed to contacting one company. CCTVs are made by a number of companies including HumanWare, Freedom Scientific, Enhanced Vision, and Optelec. All have a model that will fit the library's budget. Local distributors often may offer funding suggestions to help the library offset the cost of the equipment. Many local Lions Clubs have assisted with the purchase of CCTVs as one of their projects.

Electronic Magnifiers—On-the-Go Magnifiers

CCTVs have been in use for more than forty years, but until digital technology became refined and lower in cost, users had been relegated to using the device in a designated area, as the device needed a tabletop to support it and a monitor. Now, technological advances have given birth to small, portable devices that can travel with the user.

Some of the portable devices weigh as little as seven ounces and have the ability to magnify objects up to fifteen times (15x). The weight and magnification depend on the model chosen; the smaller it is, the less magnification is possible. The devices are easy to use, although the smaller the device, the greater the need for a steady hand, as the user is holding the device over the target. Usually, an orientation to the button functions is all that is needed for the patron to learn how to use the device.

Portable magnifiers enable patrons with low vision to browse the library stacks and independently look at titles and call numbers. The limitation is that most devices on the average will only magnify approximately eleven times (11x), and the display area is as small as four inches, and no larger than six inches, meaning that users can only view a few words at a time. However, if the library has a lot of open stacks for browsing, it may wish to pursue the purchase of a portable magnifier, as they are moderately priced and offer patrons flexibility. Figure 3.6 shows a typical portable magnifier and how compact such magnifiers can be.

Figure 3.6
Portable Magnifier

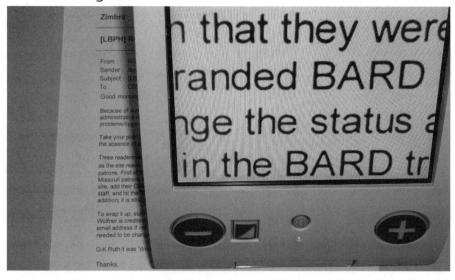

Today's portable magnifiers are lightweight and powerful and can assist patrons with low vision wherever a patron may need extra magnification.

Printers

Although most specialized printer programs offer large-print output of word documents created within the program, this option does not extend to documents found online. It is helpful therefore, if possible, to set the default printer for the large-print workstation to a sans serif large-print font (over 14 points), which will produce the clearest and easiest-to-read document. As noted earlier, not all fonts are easy to read (see figure 3.1).

Which Solution Is the Right One?

Providing large-print access for patrons is one of the least costly accommodations the library can provide, and it likely stands to be used by the most people. It can be used by low-vision patrons as well as by those with learning differences. It requires little staff assistance, as the products are fairly easy to use. Which product the library purchases should be based on the software that can best be supported by the IT Department and the staff who will be doing training. It is advisable to consult local vision-rehabilitation training centers or consumer groups to determine what product is being used in the library's service area.[12] Also, remember that old technology such as handheld magnifiers (illuminated or not) are still useful and viable options if the library has yet to move to electronic resources for text enlargement.

Notes

1. Microsoft Corporation, "The Aging of the U.S. Population and Its Impact on Computer Use," www.microsoft.com/enable/research/agingpop.aspx.

2. Ibid.

3. Eberly College of Arts and Sciences, "Strategies for Teaching Students with Learning Disabilities," www.as.wvu.edu/~scidis/learning.html; and National Center for Learning Disabilities, "Accommodations for Students with Learning Disabilities," www.ldonline.org/article/ Accommodations_for_Students_with_LD.

4. RealAge, "Aging Eyes—See into Your Future," www.realage.com/check-your -health/eye-health/aging-eye. Further information relating to specific lighting solutions can be found at Dan Roberts and Roy Cole, "Lighting for Low Vision," September 2003, www.mdsupport.org/library/lighting.html.

5. A full discussion of Microsoft's Accessibility products can be found at "Accessibility in Microsoft Products," www.microsoft.com/enable/products/.

6. To learn more about ZoomText, view a demonstration of the product, or down-load a trial copy of the software, visit Ai Squared, at www.aisquared.com.

7. For further information on MAGic for Windows, or to download a trial copy, visit Freedom Scientific's website, at www.freedomscientific.com.

8. To learn more about Dolphin, see "Who Is Dolphin?" at www.yourdolphin .com/dolphin.asp.

9. To determine the viability of Dolphin products in the library's service area, see www.yourdolphin.com/dealer_zone.asp.

10. For further information on this product, visit the Clarity Technology website, at http://getwinzoom.com.

11. Further information about the requirements to use Lazarus, as well as the product itself, may be found at www.lazarus.freepascal.org; see also Open Source Magnifying Glass, http://magnifier.sourceforge.net/#opensource.

12. In addition to consulting with the library's community rehabilitation centers, also contact the library's local chapter of the National Federation of the Blind, at www.nfb.org, and the American Council of the Blind, at www.acb.org.

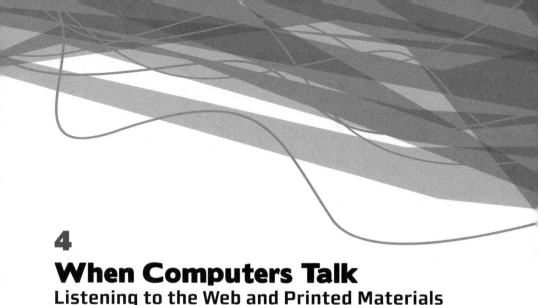

4
When Computers Talk
Listening to the Web and Printed Materials

Most people who have low vision or who are blind access computers by listening to text being read by screen-reading technology. Likewise, people with certain types of learning disabilities, such as dyslexia, are better able to comprehend when they hear printed text read aloud.[1] Additionally, some people with cognitive disabilities are empowered by access to this technology.

Screen Readers

How the Technology Works

Screen reader technology involves using software that recognizes online text and uses its intelligence to translate that text to a verbal output through synthetic speech or a refreshable Braille display. Most users opt for the verbal output although users who are avid Braille users or people who are deaf and blind will use the screen-to-Braille output option.

A screen reader is the interface between the computer's operating system, its applications, and the user.[2] Today's screen readers are robust and usually incorporate a speech synthesizer. A screen reader will recognize the words and relay the text to the synthesizer; the synthesizer will speak the words through the computer's sound card, enabling the user who cannot read the text to hear the text.

Most synthesizers are able to speak at a variety of speech rates and vocal pitches. Many offer the user a wide selection of voice options, and some even speak in languages besides English. The technology allows users to dictate how they want the text read in regard to rate of speech, pitch of the synthetic voice, and how much should be read at a time (i.e., word, sentence, paragraph, page, or the entire document). Shortcut key commands are prevalent in most screen reader programs, which enables skilled users to zip through a document with speed.

Basically, the user sends commands by pressing different combinations of keys on the computer keyboard to instruct the screen reader as to what to read and to speak automatically when changes occur on the computer screen. Key commands allow users the flexibility to perform more advanced functions, such as locating text displayed in a certain color, reading predesignated parts of the screen on demand, reading highlighted text, and identifying the active choice in a menu. Users may also access the spell-checker in a word processor or read the cells of a spreadsheet with a screen reader.

The screen reader will read all that is on the screen, including names, descriptions of buttons, menus, text, and punctuation, but the keyword here is *read.* When we see things with our eyes, we use recall to know what the object is. If the objects on-screen are not identified with an appropriate text description, their presence will not be comprehended by the screen reader. For example, if the library has a logo that defines the organization and the web designer simply identifies it as a logo, all the reader will know is that there is a graphic of the logo on the page. However, if the web designer described the logo as "library logo, book with a beacon emitting light," the screen reader will relay that information to the patron. Mozilla Firefox supports a free extension that enables site managers to view a textual representation of a web page similar to how the page would be read by a modern screen reader.[3]

Selecting a Screen Reader

It is challenging for public entities such as libraries to select products that will meet each user's individual needs or desires. Libraries are faced with the challenge of providing technology that will offer the most access for the most people without infringing on the rights of other patrons. The key thing to remember when selecting a screen reader is to ask patrons, consumer organizations, and assistive-technology vendors what is the preferred reader in the library's service area.

Although screen readers are similar in their functionality and capabilities, there are differences. For example, the keyboard shortcuts in one screen reader will rarely perform the same function in other screen readers.[4] Likewise, they also have different ways of notifying users of important information, such as which pieces of text are links, which pieces of content are images, and so forth. Regardless of reviews of the products or the cost, it is wise to select the one that has a "fan base" in the library's service area. Screen readers are a very personal choice, and there is a brand loyalty for most users as there is much time spent learning the intricacies of the software as well as the money invested in the product.[5] Selecting a preferred product will also give the library's information technology (IT) staff a knowledge base to turn to should problems arise, reduce the need to offer intensive training, and help promote the product being available in the library.

System Requirements

The most important system requirement is a staff willing to understand the process of the interface. Often this task falls to one person, which would be acceptable if that person agreed to work around the clock. Although this technology is not difficult to comprehend, it does need to be understood by more than one person.

When purchasing the computer framework for such assistive technologies as screen readers, the rule of thumb is to purchase the latest model, with the most memory, with at least two open USB ports, a large display monitor, and a high-quality graphics card. Although this may seem strange, as screen readers do not read graphics, they do "look" at all the graphics on a web page. If the graphic is identified properly, using a word description, it will be read aloud, and the user will be aware of the graphic. A more efficient graphics card will perform this task more quickly, and because screen readers cause a little drag on the processing speed, a high-end graphics card will help move the process along a little faster.

Software Programs

Software programs are relatively easy to install and offer the user a wide range of options while reading web pages or documents. Only rarely does any software problem interfere with the operating system. All of the products come with excellent documentation and support.

Job Access with Speech (JAWS)

Job Access with Speech (JAWS), a product of Freedom Scientific, is probably the most popular screen reader used today.[6] It was initially developed for computer users whose vision loss prevents them from seeing screen content. JAWS reads aloud information that is sent to the screen, and it has numerous hot-key commands, or shortcuts, which are fairly straightforward. For example, Ctrl+O opens a file. Alt+F4 will close a window. JAWS is compatible with the most frequently used office and school environment software.

In addition to performing the basic tasks of reading pages or paragraphs and announcing what it is seeing, JAWS has additional utilities that were developed in response to user requests. For example, a tool called Research It allows the user to jump to and from the Internet to a document in process by simply using a few keystrokes. Another feature is the Wiktionary, which is a web-based dictionary. The user places the cursor on a word in a document or web page, then presses the default keystroke (INSERT+WINDOWS Key+R) to quickly look up the Wiktionary definition for that word.[7]

JAWS also provides Braille output in addition to, or instead of, speech. The user must have a refreshable Braille display to use this utility (see chapter 5 for more information on Braille).[8] The Braille function works with key commands as well, with the only difference being that output is in the form of raised Braille cells and not audible output.

JAWS works well with both Internet Explorer and Firefox, and both browsers have help pages for people who are using JAWS with their product. Because of the popularity of JAWS, there are numerous tutorials available, hot-key tip sheets, and a multitude of users.[9] This latter attribute translates to it being easier for the library to find volunteer trainers to instruct new users on the product's use. It should be noted that JAWS, although being the most popular screen reader, is expensive. Many people with low incomes cannot afford to purchase it for their own home use yet are expected to know how to use the software to acquire good-paying jobs. In a very unofficial survey of libraries that have assistive technology, this is the most requested and most used product.

Window-Eyes

Window-Eyes, a product of GW Micro, is the second most popular screen reader in North America. It supports all the functions readers need to access the World Wide Web as well as all Microsoft programs, including PowerPoint and Excel. It offers support for Skype, which is unique, and has support for mobility through USB drives. A very strong feature supported through Window-Eyes is that it excels in reading PDF files, as it pioneered the utility. Window-Eyes also has a key describer mode, useful hot keys, four alternate keyboard layouts, a utility that can describe online colors, and enhanced Braille features. Key commands are logical—for example, a user wishing to locate the next link simply presses the *L* key, or to find the next header, the *H* key.

Window-Eyes works well with both Internet Explorer and Firefox, and both browsers have help pages for those people using Window-Eyes with their products.

With library funds being in short supply, it should be noted that this package is less expensive than similar products. It has all the functionality most users will require in a public setting. The product is well documented online, and tutorials and cheat sheets are available.[10]

HAL

HAL, from Dolphin Computer Access, a United Kingdom company, is a powerful screen reader that works to give both speech and Braille output. It works in harmony with a vast array of products from the Microsoft line. It is proficient in reading PDF files and has a forms utility allowing users to locate boxes that need data input. It is popular in some areas of the world, as the product has strong scripting support, which allows users to tailor products to fit their needs.

HAL offers multiple one-key command options that enable users to breeze through documents. A strong selling point for Dolphin's HAL is that it is also available as a product called Dolphin Pen, which allows users to take their software with them and have it travel from computer to computer without having to install it. In a public setting, this would enable the library to make any PC one that has screen-reading capabilities.

Dolphin Computer Access has a number of online support utilities, including tutorials and links to discussion forums, where users can find answers to their questions. For all its strength and comparable pricing, the product has spotty use in North America, although it is said to be growing with the availability of the Dolphin Pen. If there is a demand for this particular package it would be prudent to ask the vendors about the number of users in the library's service area.[11]

Serotek Corporation System Access Standalone

Another product line to consider comes from Serotek Corporation. The company was formed by users who are blind and wanted to offer others a quality product at a lower price than those in the marketplace. In their company's System Access Standalone with NeoSpeech VoiceText, they have done that.[12] System Access Standalone provides screen-reading options to use with spreadsheets, word processing, and surfing the Web. System Access Standalone provides intuitive access to all Windows-based applications. Purchase of a license allows the product to be used on up to two computers.

What You Need Now (WYNN)

What You Need Now (WYNN) is a product of Freedom Scientific and works in support of literacy enhancement for those who have a learning disability that prevents them from comprehending the text they are reading. The software (unlike most humans) is a patient companion and will repeat words and pages as many times as necessary. The learning curve is a short one, and tutorials are available.

The product has four toolbars with a point-and-click interface. There are large, intuitive universal buttons that are easy to use as they are color coded and labeled with both pictures and words. The screen reader will read the text and highlight the words as they are spoken. The user can ask for an immediate definition of any words not understood and consult a thesaurus to ensure he or she understands the word. The software also allows users to mask the amount of information they are hearing and seeing, so as to not create a sensory overload. One of the toolbars that is most useful to the user with a learning disability is the writing toolbar, which has many of the features of a word processor but also has features such as word prediction, homophone explanations, and the ability to create an outline. This last allows the user to visually organize ideas, concepts, and topics helping in the writing process. The program allows for a smooth toggling from Web to word document. Freedom Scientific offers total support for the program.[13]

Read and Write Gold

Read and Write Gold is a robust software program from Texthelp Systems, which has a strong international user base. This technology enables those with learning disabilities to comprehend what they are reading and learn through the reading experience. The program has many utilities that support easier reading for many. The software masks text, allows words to be defined as needed, utilizes word prediction, reads PDF files, and enables the user to toggle to and from the Internet as required. It also enables speech input and has a speech pronunciation tutor. The program is also being marketed as a resource for learners of English as a second language.[14]

Budget Screen Readers

If the library does not have a budget to purchase a commercial screen reader, there are some low- to no-cost options. The adage that "you get what you pay for" applies to software as well. Nevertheless, they are worth considering as they offer some access rather than ignoring the issue totally.

NVDA (NonVisual Desktop Access)

There's a relatively new software package for those with visual impairments to gain greater access to digital media, NVDA. NVDA is short for NonVisual Desktop Access, a "free and open source screen reader for the Microsoft Windows operating system."[15] The software can be installed on a host computer or run from a USB flash drive, which empowers the user with its portability. It comes with eSpeak, a free open-source multilingual speech synthesizer, and will also work with Audiologic, Display, and Silence. NVDA supports Mozilla Firefox Thunderbird and offers "basic support" for such Microsoft products such as MS Word 2003, Outlook Express, MS Excel 2003, and many other programs.

Although it could be useful to those with visual impairments, the product would not aid those with a learning disability as it does not provide a visual cue to indicate to the user what is being read.[16] It is free, however, offers portability, and is an open-source product, which means it could get better.

NaturalReader

NaturalReader is a mainstream product line developed by NaturalSoft and is one of the most reasonably priced text-to-speech systems available. There are six versions available: the Free Version, the Personal Edition, a developer edition, and three professional versions. The Free Version does not offer many utilities, but it may be enough to help patrons read documents or work their way through short articles. It will not enable users to use Internet Explorer and some word-processing programs. On the other hand, the Gold Edition has utilities such as typing echo, works with most word-processing programs, can handle large files, and offers the user the choice of several realistic synthetic voices. NaturalReader supports German, Spanish, French, Arabic, and UK English voices. Depending on the library's budget and needs, the Personal Edition and professional versions, which are more complete and priced at under $100, could be a reasonable way to place access at more locations.[17]

Microsoft Narrator

Narrator is a text-to-speech program (or basic screen reader) that is built into Windows XP, Windows 2000, Windows Vista, and Windows 7. The utilities of the product vary from version to version.

With the release of Windows 7, users are saying that Narrator is finally a usable product as it lets the user define how the reader will read the display and announces some of the events happening on the screen. Although Narrator is not an answer for those who are totally dependent on having a screen read to them for school or work, this will be of some use to the user needing to seek out some short pieces of information. Narrator is easy to launch, and Microsoft provides thorough tutorials for each version.[18] If the library cannot afford to purchase a commercial screen reader, staff should be aware of the Accessibility products offered by Microsoft and should be allowed to launch them for patrons needing them.

Mac VoiceOver

Apple's Mac supports a text-to-speech utility called VoiceOver, voiced by Alex, a natural-sounding speech synthesizer that actually pauses at appropriate places as it reads paragraphs. Users are able to control their computers using only keyboard commands. One of the strongest features of VoiceOver, however, is that personal settings can be saved on a USB drive and used on any Mac computer, eliminating the need for special workstations for persons with special access needs. VoiceOver is available through Mac's Universal Access Panel.[19]

Reading and Scanner Technology

Although more documents are becoming available electronically, there are valuable pieces of information that are still only available in traditional print format, including correspondence that is still delivered to mailboxes. Technology that can scan printed documents or graphic-based text and convert it to speech output (also large print) is a valuable tool for people with print disabilities who wish to do research or read the daily mail. The software works with a flatbed scanner using advanced optical character recognition (OCR) to scan the text and send the text to a text-to-speech software synthesizer. There are several units available.

Text-to-Speech Software

OpenBook

OpenBook scanning and reading software, a product of Freedom Scientific, is a proven and reliable device. When coupled with a scanner, it will scan documents and convert them to speech, which will be read aloud at the command of the user. OpenBook also allows the user to search for and download books and audio files from the Internet. The product works in harmony with Microsoft Word, allowing users who are blind, are visually impaired, or have a learning disability to prepare homework assignments, work documents, or correspondence. Braille users will also find support within the product.

OpenBook is a good tool for people with low vision in that font style, type size, character spacing, and colors can be easily manipulated to suit the users' needs. Among many features, the Masking and Word Spotlighting tools synchronize the text with the verbal output, making it easy to follow along.[20]

Kurzweil 1000

Kurzweil Education Systems has a long history in the field of scanning and reading technology. When connected to a scanner, the Kurzweil 1000 will scan printed or electronic text and read homework assignments or the daily mail with ease. There are utilities for browsing documents by having the first or last (or both the first and last) sentence of each paragraph read, which allows the user to quickly scan a document. The user can then choose to read the paragraph sentence by sentence or skip it. A bookmarking feature lets users mark areas they want to refer to later, and there is a note-taking feature, which the user may wish to refer to after the document is read thoroughly. Additionally, this feature will present a summary of all that is marked up along with the notes on command.

The strength of the Kurzweil 1000 is its immediate connectivity to online materials; just a simple keystroke will take the user to the Internet. The Kurzweil 1000 comes with a classic literature CD that contains hundreds of public-domain titles that can be accessed and read aloud.

Kurzweil products are well supported and documented. The parent company is well aware of legislation that affects education for students with disabilities and offers help in composing grant requests.[21]

Smart Talking Scanners

If the library's budget is nonexistent, the library may opt to go with a stand-alone scanner with speech output. Such scanners can read aloud what they scan, which opens the library's print collection to patrons with print disabilities. Books, magazines, and the patron's own correspondence go from being inaccessible to accessible.

What the scanners do not do is connect to the Internet, which could be problematic for some patrons. Staff could perform the searches and print the material, then patrons could scan the printout. This option could become time-consuming, and some patrons might take exception to the fact that someone is performing the searches for them, but it still is a viable option.

ScannaR

The ScannaR from HumanWare is easy to learn how to use; one lesson should be sufficient for most users. It is simply a flatbed scanner that can translate the printed word to a spoken word by pressing one button. After the scan, the user can opt to save the scanned materials, to reread, or delete them. It is easy for patrons to add file names to the scanned documents, as there is a built-in microphone. If saving scanned documents is a problem, the microphone would have to be disabled.[22]

Scanning and Reading Appliance (SARA)

Freedom Scientific produces Scanning and Reading Appliance (SARA), which is a reliable, sophisticated, and fairly easy-to-use device with a one-button Start command and an installed dictionary. There is a lot of flexibility in the product as users can have materials read line by line or word by word, or they can have a complete document read.

SARA also can be connected to a monitor to enable people with low vision to read scanned documents in a mode that they can see. There are thirty-five interchangeable text and monitor color combinations, plus numerous font and color options. An attribute called spotlighting helps users keep their places within documents and works with the SARA voice output. This feature could help both low-vision patrons and patrons with learning disabilities.

In addition to being a reader-scanner, SARA plays most audio formats, including Digital Accessible Information System (DAISY), which is the internationally acceptable method of formatting talking books for readers who are blind. SARA comes loaded with one hundred classic titles.[23]

Eye-Pal SOLO

There is a fairly new device in the marketplace, from a small company called ABiSee, called Eye-Pal SOLO. The product was named Eye-Pal SOLO because it reads to the user on its own—absolutely no buttons to push, nothing to adjust. All staff members need to do is plug it in, and it's ready to operate. A patron simply places a book or newspaper on the reading bed, and it starts reading. To stop Eye-Pal SOLO from reading, the user simply removes the reading material from the bed. To pause the machine from reading, all the user has to do is wave a hand near the device; to resume, another hand motion will restart it. Eye-Pal SOLO can be connected to a monitor and used as a text enlarger, as the text scanned and read will be displayed on the screen. This is a basic, easy-to-use device that will enable patrons who are not willing learners to read magazines, newspapers, and their correspondence. In addition to the basic model, there is a more advanced option.[24]

Web-Based Screen Readers

Relatively new developments in the field of voice output to Internet content are web-based applications such as Spoken-Web. These web portals are capable of managing content like news updates, weather, science information, and so forth, and adding text-to-speech functionality to the web content.[25] The primary audiences for such applications are those who have difficulty reading because of learning disabilities or language barriers.

Another portal is Browsealoud, which was created by Texthelp Systems. Texthelp Systems promotes a tool to website owners that makes their web pages audible. A links library of sites that are audible without the user having to download software is maintained on the Texthelp website.[26]

Web Anywhere (WA) is another product that provides audio output of screen contents and is restricted to the web browser.[27] WA was developed by the Computer Science Department of the University of Washington and is free. The product offers basic web browsing that includes navigation by heading, link, and input control, but it lacks many of the sophistications found in traditional screen-reading programs such as reading tables or incorporation of links. What it will do, however, is allow users who need voice output to connect to the World Wide Web or check for e-mail messages anywhere without specialized software having to be purchased. WA does caution that it is in early release and promises to improve access as soon as possible. This product would be useful to have on computer stations allocated for quick access.[28]

A Word about Browsers

When interfacing with the Internet, screen readers essentially read what they see, so it is imperative for websites to be accessible. Likewise, browsers must also be useful tools for those with some type of disability. If you cannot use the browser, you cannot surf the web. The World Wide Web Consortium (W3C), the organization that sets guidelines and standards for web accessibility, has created a standard for Accessible Rich Internet Applications (ARIA). Two popular web browsers have proven themselves to work with the most technologies as well as a text-based browser.

Internet Explorer

Microsoft, with Internet Explorer, has actively sought to offer accessibility support for Internet surfers using assistive technology. Each release of Explorer has been more usable than the last. The browser allows the user to select text and move around the web page using keyboard commands (as opposed to mouse clicks); enables the user to change the text, colors, and font size on web pages and documents; and helps locate text on web pages.

Additionally, there are options given to simplify common tasks through accessing the accelerators using keystrokes. These applications are fairly straightforward, easy to learn, and come with tutorials.[29]

Mozilla Firefox

Firefox has become a preferred browser for many web surfers, but many users of screen readers consider it an essential tool. Firefox has many "extensions" that can be installed to make browsing function better as patrons need to find ways around barriers. Extensions can do things such as make web pages more accessible or block advertisements that get in the way of accessibility. Firefox also enables the user to make the font size and button size larger or change their color. The user can turn off the Java applets or restrict what information is presented, such as pictures.

Firefox is committed to enabling screen readers to locate information with greater ease. It works with the three leading commercial screen readers and maintains dedicated accessibility information pages.[30] Additionally, several active blogs maintained by developers or expert users of assistive technologies offer tips to users and often act as conduits to Firefox developers.[31]

Lynx

Lynx is a text-only browser, and it is disability-friendly in a way that no graphical-user-interface-based browser can be.[32] By its very nature, Lynx is designed for keyboard-only interaction, with no pull-down menus, no pop-up windows, no mouse controls, and nothing to click on. In short, it cuts through a lot of the "window dressing."

The product is upgraded with fixes and modifications from the World Wide Web community. The browser is free and may be already on the library's computers. It should be bookmarked for easy access. Staff may find that patrons without disabilities may enjoy and prefer using Lynx, as it is extremely fast.[33]

Environmental Add-Ons

It is useful to have a keyboard that has some tactile surface to enable patrons to find their way around the keyboard unassisted. For persons who are totally blind, the home keys are all that need to be marked, but for those with low vision, it is helpful to have large print on the keyboard.

Although specialized keyboards can be purchased for use in conjunction with large-print screen readers, there are low-cost alternatives, such as pres-ply key tops, which can be added to the library's existing keyboards.

The large-print key displays are useful for those with some vision and those not comfortable with keyboards as well as for people with learning or cognitive disabilities. The items are low cost, easy to apply, and available from a variety of retailers offering assistive-living products. Additionally, there are versions that have large print as well as tactile surfaces.

It is also prudent to equip the workstation with headphones (with disposable covers) or earbuds. This allows the patron a sense of privacy while listening to text and keeps the noise level down in the computer area. Inasmuch as sanitation is justifiably a concern, patrons can be asked to purchase the earbuds or bring a pair from home.

A Final Word of Advice

Giving voice to the text may very well be a challenging venture, but it is encouraged, as it can be a solution for many people with print disabilities. A final word of advice is to select the solution(s) that the library can best support with staffing or volunteers. It does no good to have the software and hardware if library personnel do not know how to use them.

Notes

1. A simulation of reading with dyslexia is offered by the organization WebAIM, at www.webaim.org/simulations/dyslexia.php. The simulation demonstrates how people with dyslexia incorrectly see words and how a screen reader sees them correctly.
2. American Foundation for the Blind, "Screen Readers," www.afb.org/prodbrowsecatresults.asp?catid=49.
3. Peter Krantz, "Fangs—the Screen Reader Emulator," *Standards-Schmandards: A Problematic Approach to Web Accessibility* (blog), www.standards-schmandards.com/projects/fangs/.
4. Utah State University, "Designing for Screen Reader Compatibility" and "How Screen Readers Read Content," WebAIM, www.webaim.org/techniques/screenreader/.
5. WebAIM, "Screen Reader User Survey Results," *WebAIM Blog,* October 29, 2009, http://webaim.org/blog/screen-reader-user-survey-results/. Interesting and useful information from consumers in relation to screen readers can be accessed within this survey.
6. WebAIM's survey reported that 75 percent of users responding to the survey replied that they used JAWS software, http://webaim.org/blog/screen-reader-user-survey-results/.

7. JAWS is available from numerous dealers. To download a trial copy of the software, go to "What's New in JAWS 11," www.freedomscientific.com/downloads/jaws/JAWS-whats-new.asp.

8. A refreshable Braille display is a piece of hardware that sits alongside of the keyboard. It works in conjunction with screen-reading software to enable users to read what is on the screen. It has actuators that raise and lower to form Braille cells, which Braille readers can feel with their fingers to read what is being displayed on the screen.

9. Kathleen Beaver's *JAWS Tutorial* is designed for a sighted tutor to teach a blind user to use JAWS with Windows programs: http://atto.buffalo.edu/registered/Tutorials/jaws/index.php.

10. Cheat sheets are extremely helpful and often enough to enable staff and patrons to quickly learn a product. The Wisconsin Center for the Blind and Visually Impaired offers a host of instruction sheets that can help form the foundation of training manuals. The center supports a "Cheat Sheet for Window-Eyes" as well as a host of other products used by people using adaptive technologies at www.wcbvi.k12.wi.us/technology.new/assets/handouts/Window-Eyes%20Cheat%20Sheet.pdf.

11. Dolphin is getting a foothold in North America. To determine if there is a dealer in your area, see www.dolphinuk.co.uk/dealer_zone.asp?id=&country=198&state=999&Submit=Submit.

12. To learn more about the product, including system requirements, visit http://serotek.com/system-access-standalone.

13. WYNN is a product of Freedom Scientific's Learning System Group. The company offers online support, and the products are fully documented with tip sheets, FAQs, and system requirements. Visitors can also request free demonstration software at www.freedomscientific.com/LSG/products/wynn.asp.

14. To learn more about this product and view a video of it in use, visit the website, at http://texthelp.com/default.asp?pg_id=10250. The website also has grant-seeking tips.

15. NonVisual Desktop Access (NVDA) offers this product free of charge at http://nvda-project.org.

16. J. Howe, "Free Screen Reader for the Visually Impaired," *Associated Content Technology,* October 1, 2008, www.associatedcontent.com/article/1025898/free_screen_reader_for_the_visually_pg2.html?cat=15; and Access Technology Team, "Low-Cost Screen Readers," www.nfb.org/images/nfb/Publications/bm/bm09/bm0905/bm090506.htm.

17. NaturalReader offers an overview of its products at www.naturalreaders.com/products_compare.htm.

18. To determine which Accessibility programs the library might be able to utilize as well as to learn how the products work, see Accessibility in Windows, www.microsoft.com/enable/products/default.aspx; and see www.microsoft.com/enable/training/windowsvista/narvoice.aspx. Tutorials are available at the Microsoft site.

19. For more information on Apple's VoiceOver and other accessibility features that may assist those with visual impairments, visit www.apple.com/accessibility/macosx/vision.html.

20. Visit the website, at www.freedomscientific.com, to locate a dealer, determine system requirements, or to download a demonstration copy of the software.

21. In addition to providing information about the product and offering downloadable demo copies of the programs, the site supports free webinars and gives tips on applying for grants, at www.kurzweiledu.com.

22. For further information about ScannaR, visit the HumanWare website, at www.humanware.com.

23. To learn more about SARA, visit www.freedomscientific.com/products/lv/sara-product-page.asp.

24. To learn more about the ABiSee product, visit www.abisee.com.

25. Spoken-Web is available at www.spoken-web.com/index.cgi?p=about and does require the user to download a configuration file to use.

26. To view speech-enabled websites, visit Texthelp Browsealoud, at www.browsealoud.com/page.asp?pg_id=80098.

27. National Federation of the Blind, "Low-Cost Screen Readers," *Braille Monitor* (May 2009), www.nfb.org/images/nfb/Publications/bm/bm09/bm0905/bm090506.htm.

28. To use the program or to learn more about Web Anywhere, visit http://wa.cs.washington.edu.

29. Microsoft, "Internet Explorer 8 Accessibility Tutorials," www.microsoft.com/enable/training/ie8/default.aspx.

30. To learn more about Firefox's accessibility features, visit www.accessfirefox.org/Firefox_Accessibility_Features.php.

31. Marco's Blogspot, found at www.marcozehe.de/, and Mindforks, at http://mindforks.blogspot.com, are two.

32. Dave Taylor, "What Capabilities Does the Lynx Text-Only Web Browser Offer?" *Ask Dave Taylor,* www.askdavetaylor.com/what_capabilities_does_the_lynx_textonly_web_browser_offer.html.

33. To locate Lynx on the library's computer, try typing "which lynx" or "locate lynx." If Lynx is not found, it may be downloaded from http://lynx.isc.org. Full documentation and tips for use are also located on the website.

5
Touching the Internet
Braille Access to the Internet

After learning why speech access to PCs and the Internet is economical and user-friendly, you may feel the need to ask a simple question: Why do blind people still use Braille when they could just activate a program and hear the text read?

Braille is used by blind persons or persons whose vision is sufficiently impaired so they cannot read printed material. Braille is an extremely efficient and reliable tool of literacy for blind persons. Like a print reader, a Braille reader is aware of the spelling and punctuation of words in a document; it is the closest approximation to print for blind persons. Braille also enables a blind person to write in a form that can be immediately read. Blind persons of all ages and in all walks of life use Braille in the same ways that sighted persons use print. Learning to read Braille is much the same process as learning to read print. Only through reading words and feeling them through touch can you independently learn to spell and understand grammar.

Unfortunately, there is a decline in the percentage of new Braille readers, typically children. In the 1960s, half the population of children who were blind learned Braille and used it; today, only 12 percent are considered Braille literate. This statistic rears its ugly head when we learn that, of people who are blind and gainfully employed, 90 percent of them are Braille readers, and only 10 percent are not Braille literate.[1]

Braille advocacy groups, such as the National Federation of the Blind and the American Council of the Blind, stress the importance of Braille literacy. They support reading programs that encourage youth to read Braille and helped to pass legislation that promotes Braille education in thirty-three of the states.

Additionally, for people who are deaf and blind, Braille is the only access to printed information available.

The Basics of Braille

Braille is a tactile code that enables blind persons to read and write. It was invented by Louis Braille in 1829. Braille is embossed by hand or machine onto heavy paper and read by moving one's fingers across the top of the dots. The Braille code comprises a rectangular six-dot cell that is three dots high and two dots wide, with up to sixty-three possible combinations using one or more of the six dots. Dots are numbered from top to bottom in the Braille cell—one, two, and three on the left and four, five, and six on the right. Braille has only one set of letters. Figure 5.1 shows the Braille cell layout. By itself, a Braille letter is assumed to be lowercase. To indicate that a letter is

Figure 5.1
Braille Alphabet

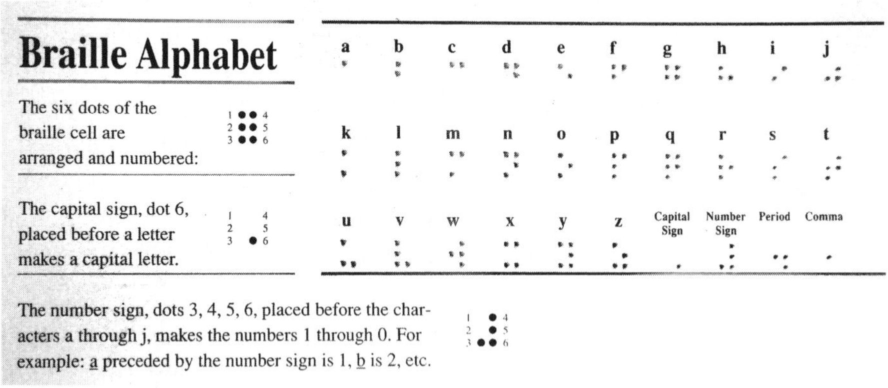

Braille provides people who are blind with the literacy skills they need to achieve equity in school and in the workplace.

uppercase, another Braille cell (the capital sign, dot six) must precede it. To show an uppercase word, two capital signs are put in front of the word. Many more symbols are in print than the sixty-three Braille symbols can represent. Most computer systems, for example, handle ninety-six different symbols.

To reduce the bulkiness of books and other documents, Braille uses a system of contractions or abbreviations. A Braille contraction is a combination of one or more cells used to shorten the length of a word. The word *mother* in Braille, for instance, would be represented by a contraction occupying only two cells rather than by spelling out the word using six cells.

There are several grades or levels of Braille. Grade 1 Braille does not contain any contractions, and it is generally used only for specialized applications where the Braille contractions might be confusing, such as in spelling lists or to acquaint new readers with the feel of the raised dots. Most students learning Braille are immediately introduced to Grade 2 Braille, which is the most common form of Braille used in North America. It uses nearly two hundred different contractions to represent capitalization, numbers, and punctuation marks. There are also Braille codes used for scientific writing and mathematics. There are nuances between the North American Braille Code and worldwide Braille codes.

A common means of teaching Braille to young students is to have the visual text interspersed with the Braille lines, as shown in figure 5.2. This allows a sighted teacher to read along with the student.

Braille Software Translators

Producing computer Braille is not as hard as it may appear. Using a software program, the command to translate from print is given, and almost instantaneously Braille cells appear that are pretty accurate, although, as Braille readers and writers will point out, only a human being can ensure 100 percent accuracy. [2] Now, the user still needs a method to get the cells beneath his or her fingertips, but this is reasonably and adequately accomplished either with a Braille display or through embossing.

Duxbury Braille Translator (DBT)

Duxbury Systems offers the Duxbury Braille Translator (DBT), a complete Braille translator and a fully functional word-processing device that supports Microsoft Windows, text files, and HTML. It is extremely easy to use for both persons who are sighted and persons who are blind. One need not

Figure 5.2
Interline Braille and Print Example

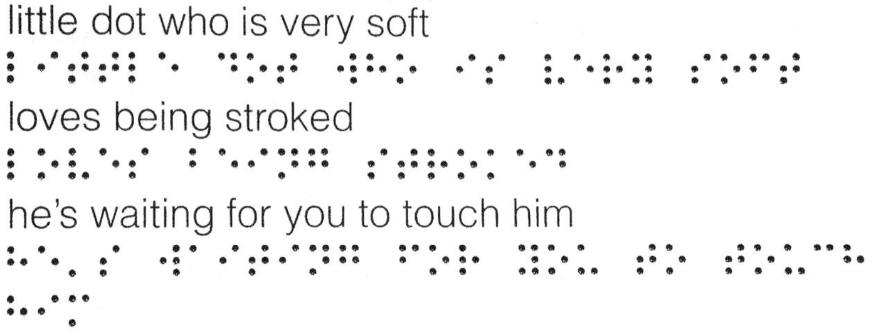

little dot who is very soft

loves being stroked

he's waiting for you to touch him

Braille and print formatting allows persons who are sighted and may not know Braille to read along with the Braille reader.

know Braille to successfully produce acceptable Braille documents (only a human can produce perfect Braille). DBT works with applications such as speech output and refreshable Braille 2 and can be downloaded to Braille embossers.

Duxbury Systems' Braille Editor allows the user to import and translate large files, with virtually no limit to the file size. Easy-to-follow, logical steps are used in the translation process, which results in excellent Braille output for the first-time user. Duxbury products also can translate text to Braille in fifty languages and can operate bilingually.

Duxbury Systems maintains an informative website with demonstrations of the company's product as well as links to many quality disability-related sites.[3]

Goodfeel Music Translator

Using a software product called Goodfeel Music Translator, from Dancing Dots, anyone can create Braille music scores without necessarily knowing Braille or Braille music. Additionally, blind musicians can learn new material prepared for them by receiving information via a multisensory experience; that is, they receive musical, verbal, and Braille information about the score, which is also displayed on the screen for sighted musicians to review in sync.[4] The program uses mainstream music-scanning programs and scripting derived from the screen reader JAWS to work. The user need not know Braille music notation to prepare Braille music scores but will need access to JAWS software. If the library is in an environment that teaches music theory, it may be beneficial to procure a copy of this software.[5] However, if the library's budget cannot support the purchase of this software, be aware that the National Library Service for the Blind and Physically Handicapped (NLS/BPH) does lend music scores to eligible registered readers of the NLS program.[6]

Displays for Braille Output

Once the Braille is translated, there needs to be a method for the user to read it—dots on a screen help no one. Braille displays provide access to the information on a computer screen by converting standard ASCII text into Braille. One option for Braille display is a raised-pin device because of the inherent high level of information and detail. In response to information from the computer, Braille is produced on the display by pins that are raised and lowered (refreshed) in combinations to form Braille characters. When used with screen-access programs, Braille displays allow users to access any portion of the screen information. All Braille displays in the United States today can show only one line of Braille and are commonly available in twelve-, twenty-four-, thirty-two-, forty-, sixty-four-, or eighty-character Braille cell configurations. Some displays are portable and battery-powered, while others are larger desktop units that typically sit under the computer keyboard.

For a proficient Braille reader, the use of a Braille display can offer many benefits over other access modes. A Braille display allows the user to move quickly from one point on the screen to any other; to skip large blank spaces easily; to note when an item on the screen changes rather than having to query the screen for the latest update; to read at a personal, often variable, rate; to observe many specifics about the text such as spelling, punctuation, and format; and to be keenly aware of items on the screen and their relative position to one another. The Braille display must accurately represent what is being shown on the computer's screen. To do this, there must be one screen character per Braille cell. Therefore, most Braille displays use a special eight-dot Braille code instead of the usual six-dot Braille cell. The presence of the additional two dots per cell allows the display to show highlighted or otherwise enhanced items. This strategy, however, does not require the user to learn a completely new Braille code.

The displayed text is usually uncontracted and written in what is called "computer Braille." Computer Braille refers to a Braille code developed by the Braille Authority of North America (BANA). This code was developed so that computer-generated symbols—such as the backslash or vertical bar—not normally found in Braille can be represented. Some experienced Braille readers may be unfamiliar with computer Braille and will need to learn a few new characters before becoming comfortable using a Braille display. Braille displays only provide output. The blind person uses a standard keyboard to communicate with the computer. A screen reader must be installed for a refreshable Braille display to work.

Integration of Speech and Braille

A computer system can have both speech and Braille access installed, and it is possible for a patron to run the access of choice. It is also possible to have speech and Braille access working together. When a coordination of speech and Braille output exists, the user has the opportunity to receive information tactilely and audibly. This approach to access combines the accuracy of Braille reading (the user "sees" what is written) and the ease of having a program speak up when there is an important message. Often, Braille users will miss error messages that flash quickly on the screen and then disappear. Speech-output systems speak the message once it appears, whether or not it has disappeared from the screen.

Considerations for Including a Braille Display in a Workstation

Librarians who are thinking of installing Braille interfaces should consider the following points when selecting the most appropriate equipment for the circumstances and also consult with potential users and a consumer database such as one maintained by the American Foundation for the Blind.[7]

> Compatibility with screen readers. Some screen reader–display combinations work better than others. Before purchasing any unit, consult the user manual from the screen reader to determine if the display is supported or simply convey to the vendor the screen reader the library owns, and ask him to guarantee that it is compatible—if he will not do this, locate another vendor.

Size of display. Braille displays vary in size. The smallest display on the market today is twelve cells, while the largest ones are more than eighty cells. A larger number of cells means that the user can read more of the computer screen at any one time without moving the Braille line to another portion of the screen. A direct and dramatic relationship exists between the number of cells and the price of the display. A forty-cell display may represent a good economic compromise.

Interface with computer system. Different models of Braille displays vary considerably in the way they will interface with a computer. Most now have USB connections, but a few require a proprietary internal card. Some models still have a serial connector.

Security and maintenance. Braille displays are very sensitive devices and are not forgiving in a busy and public environment. Braille displays usually will not withstand being dropped or having food crumbs or liquids dribbled into their interiors. The unit should be stowed when not in use. A Braille sign placed flat next to the keyboard in the accessible workstation can instruct patrons wishing the Braille display to ask for it.

Popular Braille Displays

Brailliant BrailleConnect Series
The Brailliant BrailleConnect series and BrailleConnect from HumanWare offer a wide range of options for Braille displays. All work with screen readers and Braille translators. Many are designed to be used with a laptop and are small, portable, and can run off a battery. They have Bluetooth connectivity and can connect via a USB port.[8]

ALVA Satellite 570 Pro
The ALVA Satellite line, by Optelec, a long-respected manufacturer of Braille displays, supports a wide range of displays from forty cells to eighty cells that work well with JAWS and Window-Eyes. Users of the ALVA displays like ALVA's rounded dots, whose firmness can be adjusted. They can be connected to the computer using a serial or USB connection. The displays

do not have an internal power source, so they must be plugged into a wall outlet.[9]

Focus 84

Focus 84, produced by Freedom Scientific, has a big fan base. The Focus 84 has eighty-four cells, but models are also available with forty-four and seventy cells. Braille users like the fact that the Focus models have a key configuration similar to that of a widely used device called the Perkins Braille Writer for issuing commands.[10] It runs on USB power, so no external power cord is necessary. Whiz wheels at either end of the display are used for navigation.

JAWS and Window-Eyes support for the Focus 84 are excellent. However, one reviewer noted that the rack provided for holding the computer keyboard behind the display was not reliable, necessitating that the keyboard be placed on the desk behind the display, which made for a longer reach and was less comfortable.[11]

Other Braille Display Options

Some Braille-based note takers or personal data assistants (PDAs), such as BrailleNote, PAC Mate, and Braille Sense Plus, can be used as Braille displays with both JAWS and Window-Eyes.[12] If the library's budget is limited, this is an option as it does more for the dollars spent—it can be used independently of a computer.

The major drawback of these relatively small devices is their physical size. This device is small enough to be easily slipped into a backpack, briefcase, or large purse.

BrailleNote

BrailleNote, a product of HumanWare, works as a true PDA. It allows the user to independently (without being attached to a computer) use Wi-Fi or Bluetooth to send and receive e-mail; search the Internet; perform word-processing tasks; and download and play media, including e-books in Braille or standard text. It is a versatile tool and relatively inexpensive.[13]

PAC Mate

With the PAC Mate series, Freedom Scientific supports a strong line of accessible PDAs. PAC Mates all have a QWERTY keyboard feature for inputting text. Some models may have speech input, while others come with JAWS installed.

The PAC Mates come with twenty- or forty-cell displays. The devices, when connected to a modem or Wi-Fi, allow users to surf the Internet and send and receive e-mail in addition to all Windows applications.[14]

Braille Sense Plus

Braille Sense Plus, a product of GW Micro, can best be compared to today's modern netbooks, as it is lightweight and has the full functionality of a laptop with the addition of Braille input keys and speech output. Unlike most products designed for people who are blind, this device has a viewing window that enables sighted persons to view displays as Braille users feel them. The Braille sense supports a thirty-two-cell display. The device will access the Internet using an Ethernet, wireless, or Bluetooth connection. It will work independently or can be used as the computer's Braille display. This device is loaded with additional accessories that patrons can use for downloading purposes.[15]

Braille Embossers for Printing Output

Braille access to a computer generally refers to using a refreshable Braille display. As previously described, the refreshable Braille display provides immediate interpretation of what is being displayed on the screen. However, like the sighted population, patrons who are blind may prefer to have a hard copy of the data they found. The only vehicle for output is a Braille embosser, which acts as a printer for the Braille (see figure 5.3). Should the library's budget not support the funding for an embosser, patrons should be allowed to copy materials onto a flash drive.

The price of Braille embossers has dropped significantly in recent years. However, they still are ten to thirty times more expensive than a heavy-duty standard printer. At the low end of the price range, Braille embossers produce Braille at a rate of about eighteen characters per second; at the high end, they can emboss at speeds in excess of two hundred characters per second.

Embossers can produce either single-sided or double-sided embossing. Double-sided embossing offers the advantage of conserving paper and reducing the bulkiness of a Braille printout. Until recently, the ability to emboss on both sides of a page simultaneously was reserved for the most expensive embossers. Several manufacturers of Braille embossers, however, now produce these types of embossers; they cost in the $3,000 to $4,000 price range and emboss at speeds of around forty characters per second. Although the initial

Figure 5.3
Braille Embosser

Braille embossers act as printers for Braille output, enabling Braille users to have a paper copy of information retrieved or composed.

setup of one of these embossers can be a little tricky, the good news is that they're very reliable and generally require little maintenance.

If the library does a lot of marketing in print, it may wish to consider a Braille embosser as the output can produce literature that is impressive and universally accessible. As staff proofread print productions, so should someone ensure that the Braille is error-free.

Selecting an embosser is no different than selecting a printer. Someone is going to love it, someone is going to hate it, and most will just be glad it's available. Ensure that it is compatible with the library's computer and software and that a noise shield be purchased for the embosser, as all models are loud.

ViewPlus Technologies Braille Printers

The Cub Junior and Cub Braille Embosser are from the Tiger series by ViewPlus Technologies. They produce Braille pages at a rate of thirty to sixty characters per minute and work with single sheets of paper of various widths, which do not have to be tractor fed. This is a plus, as specialized Braille computer paper is quite costly.

The embossers work with a library of Braille "images" that have been made available through a graphic studio and can be translated into tactile images. The embossers work with one-button commands and operate on Word documents as well as graphics that are produced from any PC software including Illustrator and CorelDraw. The embosser is also slightly quieter than other embossers, a consideration for the library environment. Demonstrations and further information about the embossers can be found at the ViewPlus Technologies website.[16]

Romeo and Thomas Embossers

Despite the corny names, both the Romeo and Thomas (Tommy) printer lines from Enabling Technologies provide the user with an embosser capable of rendering good-quality Braille. The Romeo 25 is the least expensive model (around $2,500) and produces Braille at the rate of twenty-five characters per second; the Romeo 40 produces Braille at a rate of forty characters per second (the price difference is about $1,000). The models have various embossing speeds, decibel-level noise outputs, and the ability to print on one side or two. If the library is green-minded, opt for a model that embosses on both sides. Enabling Technologies has video presentations of the embossers on its website and a checklist that will help libraries determine which type of embosser would best suit their needs.[17]

Index Basic D Braille Embosser

The Index Basic D Braille Embosser is produced by the Index Braille company, located in Sweden. The Index Basic D embosser is one of the most popular Braille embossers in the world. It is capable of producing double-sided embossing and produces uniform, high-quality dots. It has a built-in speech synthesizer, making it easy to install and operate for blind and sighted users alike. It does use tractor-fed, specialized paper, which cannot be purchased through an office supply company. The embosser has worldwide distribution. Further information as well as demonstrations and other system requirements can be found on the Index Braille website.[18]

Braille and the Internet Browser

No speech or Braille-access configuration will be capable of directly displaying graphically presented information; a browser is needed. Although many web surfers using Braille now use Internet Explorer or Firefox, some Braille users favor the text-based browser Lynx, as it is fast and easy to navigate. Versions of Lynx 2.5 and later support a special switch, "a show cursor," that was introduced for blind users. When the parameter "show cursor" is included on the Lynx Command line, Lynx will force the hardware cursor to follow the active link on the page. Thus, the Braille display will always show the text that is highlighted by the cursor. Although Lynx is an older browser, it still receives maintenance and is upgraded on a fairly regular basis.[19]

Braille Key Tops

It is possible to purchase Braille large-print overlay key tops for a standard keyboard. These are simply applied over the keys and offer the user a tactile reminder of which keys his or her fingers are touching. Although some Braille readers scoff at the need for the tactile keys, others who never learned to use the keyboard do need them. These key tops are available from many vendors offering assistive technologies and cost less than $25.[20]

Braille Access—A Rewarding Challenge

Providing Braille access to the Internet may seem daunting because it is specialized and expensive, but it is well worth the challenge. Although speech synthesizers yield the text presented, Braille displays are the only facility to give the user information on how the screen appears, with the exception of graphics (which are still presented as "islands"). Braille is the only real tool to fight illiteracy among the portion of the population who are blind.

Notes

1. Braille Institute, "Facts about Sight Loss: And Definitions of Blindness," *Braille Literacy Statistics,* http://brailleinstitute.org/facts_about_sight_loss#5.
2. It should be noted that the rules of Braille are complex. If the library wishes to produce information such as newsletters in Braille, the newsletters should always be proofread by a Braille reader who is well versed in the rules.
3. Duxbury Systems supports a very informative website on the history and use of Braille. Visitors can learn about Braille contractions as well as print them for instructional purposes. Visit the website at www.duxburysystems.com/products.asp.
4. William McCann, "Dancing Dots: Latest Technology and Publications" (presented to International Symposium on Braille Music Notes, November 13 and 14, 2008, German Central Library for the Blind, [DZB], Leipzig, Germany). A thorough overview of Dancing Dots products and how they work and interact with mainstream music products is explained within this paper. The document may be retrieved at www.dzb.de/req/download.php?file_id=236.
5. To learn more about the Dancing Dots product line, visit www.dancingdots.com/main/goodfeel.htm.
6. A listing of titles available can be found at the National Library Service for the Blind and Physically Handicapped, NLS/BPH Music Services, www.loc.gov/nls/music/index.html.

7. The technology database at the American Foundation for the Blind's website allows for one-stop comparison of embossers, software, and portable Braille displays; visit www.afb.org/prodBrowseCategory.asp.

8. To learn more about this product, visit the HumanWare website, at www .humanware.com.

9. To learn more about Alva embossers and to view a demonstration of one, see www.accessibleworld.org/content/demo-alva-braille-display-tek-talk-larry -lewis. The product is available from many distributors.

10. The Perkins Braille Writer can be compared to a typewriter. It has keys, and users insert paper under a roll bar to use it. However, this writer generally uses seven keys, one for each dot of a six-dot Braille cell plus a Space key. For more information, visit www.abledata.com/abledata_docs/Braille_Writers_Printers _Software.htm.

11. Susan Stageberg, "The Device That Refreshes: How to Buy a Braille Display," *AFB Access World* 5, no. 6 (November 2004), www.afb.org/afbpress/pub .asp?docid=aw050607.

12. To learn more about these products, visit HumanWare, at www.humanware .com (BrailleNote); Freedom Scientific, at www.freedomscientific.com (PAC Mate); and GW Micro, at www.gwmicro.com (Braille Sense Plus).

13. Further information, including system requirements, may be found at www .humanware.com/en-usa/products/blindness/braillenotes.

14. For more information relating to the PAC Mate series, visit www.freedomscientific .com/fs_products/PACmate_qx400.asp.

15. To learn more about the Braille Sense Plus, visit www.gwmicro.com/ Braille_Sense/FAQ/.

16. For further information about the ViewPlus Technologies Braille printers, see www.viewplus.com/products/braille-printers/desktop-braille-printers/.

17. Enabling Technologies produces and distributes a full line of embossers. For further information, visit www.brailler.com.

18. Index Braille has been producing the Basic D model, which is a double-sided embosser (embosses on both sides of the paper), for several decades. To view informative videos about the product, visit www.indexbraille.com/Products/ Embossers/Basic-D.aspx.

19. The Lynx browser can be downloaded from the Lynx support organization at http://lynx.isc.org/current/.

20. The manufacturer of the most popular brand made in the United States is Hooleon. Its website is www.hooleon.com.

6
Seeing the Sounds
Technologies for Persons with Hearing Impairments

Persons who are deaf or hard-of-hearing find the ready availability of personal computers and electronic communications as equalizers in a hearing community. Programs such as e-mail and word processing enable persons with hearing impairments to use visual methods to communicate with the hearing community. In fact, this community, in a sense, used a precursor to text-messaging technology when the Text Telephone or Text Teletype (TTY/TDD) device was established. The difference between them is that TTY/TDD technology is designed for synchronous conversation.[1] The device, still in use, works with telephone networks (including cellular networks) and enables people who are deaf, hearing impaired, or verbally impaired to communicate by typing messages using abbreviations similar to those found in e-mail, with the major exception of the letters TTYS.[2]

Because of the visual nature of computer displays, the major problem hearing-impaired users face when using computers is not being able to hear alert signals given by some programs to indicate attention by the user is needed. These problems are easily circumvented by providing people who are deaf or hard-of-hearing with access to applications that would make these sounds visually. These are often included in operating systems or are available as shareware. Other people who are hard-of-hearing may only need headphone amplifiers, which increase the volume of the notifications to an audible level and block out background noise.

There is, however, a disturbing trend in web development that stands to create access barriers for people who are deaf or hard-of-hearing. Streaming video and wave applets are being added to websites as a way to engage visitors; however, these applets are hindering this group of people from fully being part of the learning process. This could be avoided by simply following the World Wide Web Consortium (W3C) guidelines, which include captioning the spoken word and ensuring that any website the library points to for information also follows the guidelines (the W3C guidelines are discussed in chapter 2). YouTube, for example, supports captioning, so if the library is moving programming information to YouTube, be sure to caption it.[3]

Another trend that is causing access barriers is the willingness to podcast events. Libraries and other educational institutions are communicating programs through podcasts. Generally, podcasts by their nature are not accessible to the deaf, but if they support transcripts of the spoken word, they immediately become accessible.

Making System Sounds Visible

There are visual notification programs available within all Microsoft Accessibility packages that are easy to activate and easy to use. Depending on the edition of Microsoft Windows used, they are called by a variety of names:

- Show Sounds
- SoundSentry
- Visual Notification
- Display Text Alternative

Apple's Mac systems have a similar program, called Flash.

Basically, what the programs do is replace system sounds that are important to the user with visual cues, such as a flash on the screen, so that system alerts are noticeable even when they're not heard. The "display text" option replaces sound alerts with words on the screen to indicate that activity is happening within the computer. There is no charge for these programs, but staff members need to be aware of what they are, who they are designed to assist, and how to access and use them. Microsoft and Apple provide tutorials on all of the versions of the sound-to-vision products.[4]

Communication between Staff and Patron

Some of the problems deaf or hearing-impaired patrons will experience have nothing to do with the computer itself. Instead, the problem centers on communicating with the staff, who are used to being heard when conducting the in-person or telephone reference interview. There are technologies available that can assist with those communications.

Sorenson Video Relay Service

Sorenson Video Relay Service (SVRS) is a free twenty-four-hour service for the deaf and hard-of-hearing community that enables persons who know sign language to conduct video relay calls with family and friends as well as conduct everyday business with contacts such as the library. The SVRS allows those who use American Sign Language (ASL) to place phone calls to any hearing person and conversely allows hearing persons without knowledge of ASL to contact persons who do.

Sorenson offers nonprofit organizations that provide services to patrons who are deaf or hard-of-hearing, such as libraries, free SVRS equipment consisting of a Sorenson VP-200 videophone and the hardware needed to hook the videophone to the organization's Internet connection. Additionally, Sorenson will install the videophone and train staff how to use it.[5] More information on Sorenson is available in chapter 12.

Skype Video

Skype is software that allows persons to converse using the Internet and to share files with friends and colleagues worldwide. The conversations can take place audibly or visually (or both) and through instant messaging (IM). When using a quality webcam and a high-end monitor, people who converse using ASL or who lip-read can converse independently and without a fee when contacting other Skype users.[6]

Libraries that support public telephones should consider adding this feature to a workstation to enable patrons to make important connections. The same or similar time restraints could be invoked as on workstation use, and the library's communications staff would configure the unit to only allow for Skype-to-Skype calls.

Personal Digital and Assistive-Listening Devices

The personal listening devices that assist persons who are hard-of-hearing, as well as those systems designed to use in meeting rooms, have been in existence for a few decades. Basically, the person needing sound amplified wears a receiver, while the person speaking talks into the transmitter. The signals travel wirelessly from the speaker to the receiver and are good for conversation and will also work for smaller programs whereby the speaker and the receiver are no farther than ten feet apart. The signal does not travel much farther than this. This technology is a great way to conduct a one-on-one reference interview as well as one-on-one computer training with patrons with hearing impairments.

Figure 6.1
Personal Listening Device

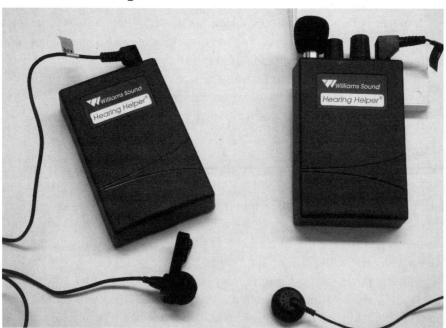

The personal listening device will allow staff to better communicate with persons with hearing loss.

These devices were invented and used for many years on an FM (radio waves) platform but are moving to digital formats. This means that the clarity is improved and the performance can be adjusted with more latitude. Personal listening devices are economical and can be purchased from companies that sell assistive technologies for the hearing impaired. An example of a personal listening device is shown in figure 6.1.

Increasing the Volume for Library Programs

The personal listening devices are just that—good for personal listening, but they generally will not work well in situations where there are a lot of people. There is a need to equip the library's meeting and program rooms to enable the sounds to be transmitted from the speaker to wherever the patron needing the hearing enhancement is sitting. To date, there is not a digital system available.

Several available technologies can be used:

> The FM technology system, whereby the sound travels by radio waves from transmitter to speaker.
> The IR or infrared system, which transmits sounds by invisible light beams from the speaker to the receiver. For this technology to be effective, the receiver must be within direct line of sight of the light beam from the transmitter.
> The audio induction or L or Loop system, which uses the principle of electronics called electromagnetics.

There are personal preferences as to which system is used, and the FM system is popular for midsize meeting rooms. People experienced in using all three technologies caution that both the Loop and IR systems may create sound "spillover."[7] The library's information technology (IT) and facilities staff, working with the deaf community, will need to determine which one will work best in the given space and the given budget.[8]

Sign Language Translator—The iCommunicator

If the library is in a community that affords it the opportunity to serve many hard-of-hearing or deaf patrons, it may wish to consider purchasing an iCommunicator. The iCommunicator uses speech-recognition software to translate the spoken word into sign language. This device has the potential to make all of the library's programming accessible to the deaf and hard-of-hearing community.

The software, working in real time, turns spoken English into text and sign language that a deaf person can view on a computer screen or display monitor. Although it appears that there is a live interpreter doing the signing, it comes from a series of video clips the patented software strings together. It is possible to have a two-way communication, as the deaf person types responses and a computer-generated voice speaks the typed words.

In addition to translating type to sign language, the iCommunicator can also translate speech to text and text to a computer-generated voice. These attributes are also helpful for persons with the inability to speak or for those with learning disabilities that are helped by seeing words displayed while spoken.

Although this technology is not inexpensive, it is unique and useful in a multiuser environment and would be technology that could be funded through grants.[9] This technology would definitely generate great publicity for the library and could be used by schools to demonstrate diversity.

Mainstream Communication Options

Readily available, existing utilities can facilitate the communications between the hearing and the hearing impaired. There is not a cost involved for their use, and staff members simply need to be aware of them and use them.

Word Processors

If the library is not in a position to purchase assistive technology at the present time for in-person communication, staff should be reminded to take advantage of the technology that is part of every library—personal computers and word-processing software. Staff can direct patrons to a workstation, where both the staff and patron can easily view text displayed on the monitor and type messages back and forth.

Paper and Pencil or Pen

Staff can also use paper and pencil or pen to write messages to the patrons; however, be prepared for the inevitable illegible note. When not writing, staff should always look directly at the patron when speaking, as that also aids communication.

Instant Messaging

Although not the best alternative and frowned on by many people in the field promoting instant relay technologies, texting can be used. Be aware that you are seeing and sending chunks of information rather than single words, so the conversation process is diminished.[10]

The Invisible Disability

Persons who are deaf or hard-of-hearing are often said to have an invisible disability as they usually walk unassisted and have no visible signs of having a disability. Do not assume a person who doesn't respond when he or she is approached is being rude; the person just may not hear. Also, be aware that some older hard-of-hearing people find that libraries are intimidating places, as they were taught that libraries are "quiet places" where "quiet voices" are to be used. They need to realize it's OK to speak up and be heard.

Notes

1. PhoneScoop.com provides a "TTY/TDD Definition" at www.phonescoop.com/ glossary/term.php?gid=259. The devices are available for purchase from dealers of assistive equipment.
2. TTYS, when used in e-mail and instant messaging, means "talk to ya soon," according to Internetslang.com, www.internetslang.com/TTYS .asp. For TTY/TDD users, it means Telecommunication Device for the Deaf or Telephone Typewriter. TTY is the most common form used for teletypes. The European community uses the term *textphone* (http://en.wikipedia.org/ wiki/Telecommunications_devices_for_the_deaf).
3. WGBH, Media Access Group, "Caption Services Captioning FAQs," http://main.wgbh.org/wgbh/pages/mag/services/captioning/faq/.
4. Information relating to product names can be found at "Comparison of Accessibility Features in Various Versions of Windows," www.microsoft.com/ enable/products/chartwindows.aspx. Tutorials for all versions of sound-access programs may be found at Accessibility tutorials for Microsoft products, www .microsoft.com/enable/training/default.aspx. Information relating to Apple's Mac Flash utility may be found on the Apple-Accessibility Hearing page, www.apple.com/accessibility/macosx/hearing.html.
5. A relay system works like any translating system involving real people. A person versed in sign language and who can hear will translate into the appropriate mode what is being communicated. Demonstrations of the Sorenson

Relay as well as more information regarding the system—including information about applying for a free system—can be found on the Sorenson website, at www.sorensonvrs.com.

6. Additional information about Skype and suggested equipment needed to effectively use Skype video can be found on the Skype website, at www.skype.com/allfeatures/videocall/.

7. Jonathan O'Dell, "Providing an Accessible Library Experience for Deaf and Hard-of-Hearing Individuals" (presentation at ALA, ASCLA, "Universal Design: Best Practices," January 15, 2010, in Boston, Massachusetts).

8. A comprehensive overview of meeting-room listening systems can be found on the Harris Communication website under "Assistive Listening, Frequently Asked Questions," at www.harriscomm.com/catalog/hcfaq/FAQald.php.

9. Demonstrations of the product and further information, including language the library can use to apply for grants, can be found at the iCommunicator's website, at www.icommunicator.com/productinfo/.

10. Arnoud vanWijk, "Real-Time Text, a Major Leap Forward for Accessible Internet for People Who Are Deaf/Hard of Hearing" (presentation at IGF, November 16, 2009, Sharm El-Sheikh, Egypt). Presentation available at www.itu.int/dms_pub/itu-t/oth/06/2A/T062A0000010003PPTE.ppt.

7
Surfing the Internet with a "Different" Board

Access problems to computers by persons with physical or mobility disabilities are often caused by their inability to manipulate a standard keyboard or mouse. For this discussion, the individuals under consideration have the ability to learn how to use the technology but need a different method for interfacing with the physical computer. Be aware that what will work for one individual may not work for another, as the degree of ability and disability will vary, as will the assistive technology that will be useful. Finding the perfect solution for each individual in the public arena may not be possible, and compromises may be necessary.

Computer Input Options

Although it does not seem as though it takes a great amount of coordination to simultaneously press Ctrl, Alt, and Del to reboot a computer, for a person who lacks the ability to use both hands, it is almost impossible. Adaptive hardware and software devices can help persons with physical disabilities access computers.

Computer input devices allow persons who have control of a single muscle (a toe, a finger, an eye) to communicate and exchange information. Some of these devices are highly specialized and will be of use to extremely small populations of persons with specific and varying degrees of disability.

Although it is not feasible to purchase every conceivable type of alternative input device, staff should be aware of the items that are available to enable them to direct patrons and their families to possible solutions. For example, if a patron only has control of a foot, there is a mouse that will allow him or her to use computers; if a patron only has control of a little finger, this patron can independently use a computer via a touch pad.

Beyond the Standard Keyboard

As stated previously, disabilities that prohibit physically handicapped persons from accessing computers are varied. Some people's only physical disability is the inability to access more than one side or one key of the computer keyboard at a time, which inhibits them from using, for example, an application program that calls for the user to press Ctrl and Enter to define a hard page. Or some people may not be able to lift their hands from the keyboard quickly enough to not cause a stroke to be entered repeatedly.

There are free software programs to enable commands that require the use of two hands as well as programs that help alleviate key repeats when a key is held down too long. The good news is that such assistance is available through software that most libraries already own.

Microsoft's Accessibility Tools

Microsoft Corporation added several features to its Windows suite of products that make it easier for people with disabilities to use computers. The feature availability varies with the version of Windows being used. Later versions of Windows have an Ease of Access Center, which will instruct the user as to what utilities are available as well as provide tutorials in their use. It is also possible to see the search utility with Microsoft's Enable website to determine which features are available on the library's software.[1] Staff should be made aware of what tools are at the disposal of their patrons and how to activate them, as they are useful and readily available. Whenever possible, shortcuts for them can be positioned on the computer's desktop. Most versions include the following tools, which are easy to turn on and off:

> **"StickyKeys"**—Simulates the simultaneous pressing of key combinations, such as Shift+Ctrl+Alt, by allowing the user to press one key at a time.

"FilterKeys" (also called **"Bounce Keys"** and **"Repeat Keys"**)— Tells the Windows program to ignore brief or repeated keystrokes accidently activated by pressing a key too long. The user tells the program what time frame to use for ignoring a depressed key.

"ToggleKeys"—When activated, signals the user with tones when keys such as Caps Lock, Num Lock, or Scroll Lock are inadvertently engaged or disengaged. This is useful if the user's fingers or hands have a tendency to drift toward the keys when resting.

"MouseKeys"—Enables the user unable to use a mouse to use the numeric keypad of the keyboard and the arrow keys to move the mouse pointer. For instance, pressing </> will simulate the left mouse click, and pressing <+> is used to simulate a double click.

Apple's Accessibility Tools

Apple's Universal Access utilities for the Mac provide powerful tools for persons who have difficulty using computers because of impaired physical motor skills. The suite of programs, part of Apple's Snow Leopard package, includes the following tools:

"Slow-Keys"—Changes the sensitivity of the keyboard to filter out unintended multiple keystrokes.

"Sticky Keys"—Simulates the simultaneous entering of key combinations, such as Ctrl+Opt+Cmd, allowing users to enter one keystroke at a time.

Alternative Keyboard Layouts—Enables users who have difficulty moving their hands across the keyboard to redefine the keys and relocate them to a location they can more easily reach.

Adjustable Key Repeat and Delay—Enables users to adjust the time span that a key will repeat if held down.

Multi-Touch TrackPad Gestures—Enables users to use swipe, pinch, and touch gestures with the TrackPad to launch applications and utilities and open documents.

Keyboard Shortcuts

Microsoft and Apple have a long history of providing an extensive grouping of keyboard shortcuts, which are combinations of two or more keys that, when pressed, can be used to perform a task that would typically require a mouse or other pointing device.[2] Keyboard shortcuts can make it simpler for people who cannot easily interact with a mouse to interact with the computer, saving time, minimizing effort, and avoiding frustration when working with Windows and the Internet. Check the menus of programs for shortcuts. For example, if a letter is underlined in a menu, that usually means that pressing the Alt key in combination with the underlined key will have the same effect as clicking that menu item.

The list of the more frequently used shortcuts should be compiled into a readable list and placed at the workstation. Patrons without disabilities may also find these shortcuts useful.

Modifications for Standard Keyboards

A few adaptations can be purchased for approximately $50 that will allow users with mobility impairments to use the standard computer keyboard. These users need the adaptations for various reasons: one patron may have poor muscle control, while another using a mouthstick may not be able to isolate the key he or she wants.[3] Although these devices will not allow the user to move through searches as quickly as one could with a special keyboard, they make access less frustrating.

Keyboard Size

Several different types of keyboards currently are available that enable the user with limited hand or wrist movement to access the computer for information. Typically, these patrons would be able to read the screen, but for some reason (arthritis, cerebral palsy, neurological damage) they cannot physically type commands on a standard keyboard to give directions to the computer. There are simple ways to solve the keyboard-access problem, and most are easily installed and cost generally around $100 or less. Although it is impossible to purchase them all, be aware that they do exist.

Oversize Keyboards

Oversize, or large, keyboards are good for people who have limited dexterity or limited ability to control their fingers as well as for people who simply

Figure 7.1
Oversize Keyboard

Oversize keyboards allow persons who have limited dexterity or who have larger hands to more accurately depress the keys they select.

have large hands. The keys generally are larger, and users have better results in finding and pressing the correct key. Figure 7.1 illustrates an oversize keyboard.

BigKeys LX
BigKeys LX, by the BigKeys Company, is an alternative keyboard that will help those with cognitive, learning, physical, and vision disabilities. All of the keys are one-inch square. All special characters of the standard keyboard are included, with the exception of the numeric keypad. BigKeys is available as Yellow BigKeys, which offers the user bright yellow keys with black print. This is a combination often recommended for people with visual impairments as well as for some users with learning disabilities. The keyboard is relatively inexpensive and comes with a good support system and a five-year warranty, all good attributes for a public library setting.

The Keys-U-See USB
The Keys-U-See USB, a product of the Key Connection, is a large-print computer keyboard that was designed for those who have a cognitive or learning disability as well as for those who have a hard time seeing the existing commands on the standard keyboard because of a vision problem. These

economically priced keyboard key tops have 41-point type on them and use high-contrast yellow keys with black printing. The keyboard also is equipped with an e-mail hot key and Internet connection key. This keyboard is available from vendors of assistive technologies as well as through mainstream vendors, such as Amazon.com.

Kinder Board

A bright and cheery keyboard such as Kinder Board, developed by Chester Creek, would be a welcome addition for persons with some types of learning or cognitive disabilities (be aware it might be disastrous for others). It is a color-coded keyboard that uses different colors to identify consonants and vowels and punctuation. The type on the oversize keys fills the entire facing of the key, making it easier for persons with limited dexterity to find their target.

Small Keyboards

Smaller keyboards are for those people who cannot expand their hands or move their fingers to reach rows of keys. All the keys need to be closer to their natural reach. There is really only one specialized vendor for the smaller keyboards, Solidtek USA (see appendix A for more information). However, because of the need for connectivity by a growing population using smart phones and other portable electronic devices, many small keyboards are now widely available.

Magic Wand

Although Magic Wand, by In Touch Systems, may not give the user the ability to summon a prince or princess, it will allow a user with little hand or head movement to fully access computers. The keyboard works with the touch of a wand, requiring no strength, and has a built-in mouse. All keys are within a 6.5-by-3-inch typing reach, and virtually no pressure is needed to depress the keys. This is a high-end keyboard that comes with a high-end price tag, but there isn't an equivalent product. If the library is in an area that has patronage needing this type of access, Magic Wand is worth the purchase price, as it is so easy to use that staff training will be minimal.

Miniature Keyboards

Although they were originally designed for users with disabilities that require one-handed typing, at 8.75 by 4.1 by 0.6 inches there are a multitude of ultra-mini keyboards being promoted for travelers and for those seeking an ergonomic keyboard for small personal computing devices. Mainstream vendors such as Qtronix Corporation, Keysonic, and Solidtek USA, to name a few, promote these very small keyboards, which were designed to work with laptops, personal data assistants (PDAs), and cell phones. Most will help a significant part of the population needing smaller keyboards. Try to acquire one that has an easy-to-locate and easy-to-use mouse emulator. The great thing about these keyboards is that they are so economical, the library can afford to buy several and let the patron use one that is comfortable for him or her. A specialized small keyboard is shown in figure 7.2.

IntelliKeys

One of the most unique, useful, and respected input products in the marketplace of assistive technology is IntelliKeys, by IntelliTools, a Cambium Learning Technologies Company. IntelliKeys has a computer-access solution for persons who have a wide variety of disabilities. The IntelliKeys keyboard is easy to install; all that is needed is a port.

IntelliKeys is seen by professionals who work with people with disabilities as an educational "equalizer." It enables users who are unable to see and communicate in traditional manners to have the ability to interface

Figure 7.2
Small Keyboard

Mini keyboards enable persons who, for example, can only use one hand to have access to the entire keyboard.

with information in a way that "makes sense" to them. This includes users who have visual impairment, cognitive impairment, mobility problems, or an autism spectrum disorder.

The keys are large and well spaced for good physical access by users with limited dexterity. They are designed using contrasting colors to enhance visual access. This keyboard tolerates a wide variety of input devices, which will interface with a standard overlay, configured for input needs of the user. The overlay is bar-coded and activated when placed on the IntelliKeys board. One of the standard overlays, for example, was designed for the user who cannot use a mouse; IntelliKeys comes with standard arrows, allowing the user to move the cursor in any direction. Another feature added for the user who cannot press two keys simultaneously is the capability to press them sequentially. IntelliKeys allows adjustment of the response to pressure on keys in a situation where a user may drag his or her fingers, activating unwanted symbols, as well as the ability to adjust the repeat rate for the user who cannot lift and move the fingers off the keys quickly.

Should the library purchase this item, staff will have to be aware of the overlays that are available and their target audience. Although IntelliTools itself offers wide support, the University of Buffalo's Assistive Technology Department offers easy-to-follow tutorials for both basic installation and use of IntelliKeys as well as for the advanced use of the product.[4]

Mouse Emulators

Certain individuals have mobility disabilities that prevent them from using any type of mouse although they may be able to grasp other items and manipulate them. They do not benefit from software that simulates mouse actions. This group of people needs a device that will emulate mouse actions. A variety of items work well and will help individuals to exploit their personal abilities to their fullest advantage.

Trackballs

Sometimes called an upside-down mouse, trackballs can be found in mainstream technology as well as in specialized assistive-technology arenas. The sophistication and applications vary. If the library's budget is limited, information technology (IT) staff may be able to find a usable trackball from one of the library's suppliers.

Wave Wireless Switch-Adapted Trackball

A product of AbleNet, the Wave Wireless Switch-Adapted Trackball, also called the Wireless Wave, acts as a mouse emulator and a switch interface. It is a plug-and-play device that works with most computers. It is designed for users with limited hand control, motor skill difficulty, hand-eye coordination challenges, and involuntary muscle spasms. The Wireless Wave features an oversize trackball that will activate with the lightest of touches.

BIGtrack

For patrons with little or no fine motor control, there is a three-inch trackball device called BIGtrack, made by Infogrip. The trackball is sturdy; it's a bright yellow color, which is easily seen; and it can withstand use in a public environment. In addition to being a trackball device, it has left-click, right-click, and drag-lock features for those able to use these functions.

Kensington Expert Trackball

Kensington Computer Products Group is a longtime fixture in the trackball community. The company continues to produce quality products and does not rest on its laurels. It continues to improve its products, and in doing so, it wins awards for innovation. The ball of the Kensington trackball is the largest available. The product has a unique design, as it incorporates a scroll ring, which enables people to move the ring with their fingertips.

L-Trac High-Performance Trackball

The L-Trac high-performance laser optical trackball, a product of Clearly Superior Technologies, has a natural contour shape that enables the user to grip it and control its actions. The device is based on laser navigation technology, and as a result, it produces a predictable, quick, and precise motion that becomes intuitive in a few minutes of use. It is well designed and is used in gaming as well, making it a good option for the rigors of public use.

Joysticks

Joysticks are an essential tool for gamers and have been for a generation. The technology allows easier maneuverability. Often, all that is needed is a tip of the stick to the left or right, and movement is made. This technology enables some with limited physical strength to move the cursor and input commands.

SAM-Trackball and Joystick

The SAM-Trackball (Switch-Adapted Mouse), distributed by RJ Cooper and Associates, was designed to be used with personal switches and will help users access computers. The device enables persons with gross-motor hand control or fine-motor head control to move the mouse, click, and double-click with whichever part of their body can be controlled.

The same technology used for the SAM-Trackball is also available as a joystick. When the user pushes the stick, the cursor does not fly off; rather, it moves in the direction pushed and at a given speed. Joysticks have worked well with users who do not have defined motor skills.

Both SAM technologies are "plug and use," but it is more than likely that the person requesting a SAM-Trackball would be highly technologically literate.

Roller II Joystick

The Roller II Joystick, which is also available as a roller ball, is a product of Traxsys Input Products, a manufacturer of assistive and mainstream input devices. The Roller II Joystick allows users with severe motor impairments to locate and input information. It comes in either a large 2.5-inch trackball or a 3-inch joystick. Each has separate buttons for left click, right click, and drag lock, with color-corresponding switch ports on the back of the units. A flashing light indicates the drag button has been activated. The Roller II products include a key guard to help users isolate the buttons. The joystick comes with two alternative handles—T-Bar and Soft Sponge Ball—to accommodate different input needs. The joystick can be outfitted with several handles to allow users a more comfortable and usable fit.

Unique Mice

Although someone with a disability may not be able to use a conventional mouse, he or she may be able to use a mouse that was developed for targeted audiences.

Senior Mouse

The Senior Mouse was designed by the German company INCAP and is shaped to fit the curvature of the entire hand to ensure a secure grip.[5] Should the user have trembling in his or her hand, the motion is counterbalanced so that uncontrollable movements do not affect the mouse. This is especially useful for individuals with upper-extremity disabilities, neurological disabilities, arthritis, cerebral palsy, multiple sclerosis, muscular dystrophy, and carpal tunnel syndrome. This is an important device to consider if there is a large senior population using the library's computers in addition to those with disabilities. See figure 7.3 for an illustration of the Senior Mouse.

Zero Pressure Finger Mouse
The Zero Pressure Finger Mouse, by Special Needs Computer Solutions, is 100 percent optical, with no moving parts.[6] The device has arrows for cursor positioning, left and right buttons, and a separate key for one-touch double clicking, as well as a Fast key for quicker traversing. If the library is looking for a unique product that will come with boasting rights, while being low cost and easy to install, this device may be it.

Zero Tension Mouse
The Zero Tension Mouse was developed to help prevent injuries and to help those who have disabilities caused by factors like carpal tunnel syndrome to use computers pain-free. The mouse allows the user to relax the hand, shoulder,

Figure 7.3
Senior Mouse

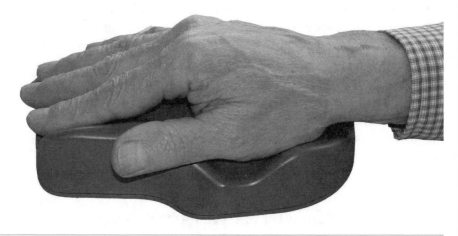

Ergonomically designed, the Senior Mouse affords the user stress-free physical access to the computer.

and neck. The mouse is a mainstream item, and it is relatively low cost. Its one drawback is also its strong suit: one size does not fit all users, and it is available in several sizes. The product is available from a multitude of vendors of ergonomic products as well as mainstream resources such as Amazon.com.

Touch Pads

With laptops, PDAs, and netbooks being a part of both our office and home lives, there are many touch pads in the mainstream technology area. Many of these may be able to work for patrons with disabilities. When looking for such a product, determine how much control is ceded to the user. For example: Can users use a light tap to enter commands? Can they run a finger across the pad for input simulation?

Cirque Easy Cat, Cirque Smart Cat, Smart Cat PRO

Cirque Corporation was developing innovative technology long before PDAs and laptops were in vogue. The three touch pad versions by Cirque Corporation are available to give people unable to use a mouse a device that will yield total mouse emulation. The user slides his or her finger across the pad, then gently taps on the pad or clicks one of the buttons to perform all mouse functions. Hot links are provided to perform repetitive functions. The touch pads vary in price and utilities.[7]

Jelly Bean Switches

Jelly Beans, by AbleNet, are 2.5-inch brightly colored flat discs that can be used to emulate mouse clicks.[8] These are switches; a switch is a broad term used for a myriad of assistive devices that replace a keyboard or replace the mouse's left click and right click. The Jelly Beans are inexpensive and useful for people who can only press downward on an object. They also work well for those with cognitive disabilities who can more easily understand that depressing the red jelly bean will let you cut, paste, copy, change the font, and so forth. The switches are low cost, are widely available, and can be used within a Wi-Fi environment. Figure 7.4 shows a Jelly Bean switch.

Software: The Computer and Web Access Suite

AbleLink Technologies developed and supports programs that enable people who cannot use traditional means to input information to access the Internet to receive and send e-mails. The software enables the user to use pictures

Figure 7.4
Jelly Bean Switch

Jelly Bean switches are used in place of a mouse by persons who are only able to press a disc or by people who find computer mice confusing.

and audio prompts to access the utilities he or she needs from a simplified Windows desktop.

The Computer and Web Access Suite comes with a total of three programs: Web Trek (a simplified web browser that actually fits directly over the Windows desktop and provides a simplified, customizable interface for users with special cognitive needs); Web Trek Connect (a specialized e-mail client that uses a picture-based e-mail system with audio capabilities for recording and sending messages; the system automatically "reads" incoming messages aloud); and Discovery Desktop (a custom Windows desktop that is easier to use as there are just the basics with less clutter).

The suite is economically priced, comes with a good support system, and will be a boon for those with cognitive disabilities who cannot read and understand traditional text. AbleLink Technologies does allow potential customers to try it out before they buy it.[9]

Touch Screens
Touch screen technology is a mainstream technology that is used in places like airports or restaurants to enable customers to serve themselves. This

technology is intuitive and easy to use and also is good for persons with cognitive impairments or autism spectrum disorders. Touch screen technology removes the ambiguity that occurs when operating the mouse, using a keyboard, or making any other type of inputting and computer responses. In other words, no "middle-technology" interface is interpreted.

Some individuals with physical disabilities who cannot use other types of pointing or input devices may also benefit from touch screen technology. In addition to the mainstream products, several products specifically designed for audiences with special needs are also available.

EdMark TouchWindow

A specially designed touch technology is the EdMark TouchWindow, which enables users to move text and operate pull-down menus with the touch of a finger. Once the software is installed and the TouchWindow is placed over the standard fifteen- or seventeen-inch monitor, the user can access electronic information. This product is available from a number of assistive-technology vendors. It is suggested that the library's IT staff conduct an interview with vendors to ensure compatibility with the library's operating system.

Microsoft Window Touch

Available with Vista and Windows 7, Window Touch is a utility that enables users who also have computers with multitouch technology to move items around by simply touching their fingers to the screen and moving it. Files can be moved, utilities activated, and documents flipped through, all by moving the fingers. The system is still in a Windows environment, however, and may not help persons with cognitive impairments. It may help persons with physical impairments use computers more efficiently.

Virtual or On-Screen keyboards

Virtual keyboards for this discussion are those that exist on a monitor rather than in a physical form. The keyboards, which are displayed on-screen, allow persons using switches, alternate trackballs, or mouse emulators to use computers by pointing at the display and resting on a key for a set amount of time. A patron who is quadriplegic may actually only be able to control his or her head. Such patrons can use tracking technology that will allow them to move the cursor from key to key, hovering for a few seconds on the correct key to signal the key is correct.[10] Several on-screen keyboard packages exist, and some are now available free of charge from shareware sites.

WiViK

One of the oldest and most effective and respected virtual keyboard products is the one offered by WiViK. It enables persons who are using a variety of switches to access Windows-based programs. All on-screen keys work just as they would if one were typing on a physical keyboard. The user selects a key, and WiViK sends it to a word processor; the same extends to sending an e-mail message or finding a web page or other text-based application. Keyboards can contain any keys the user wants, can be moved anywhere on the screen, and can be any size. The technology provides the user with the ability to hear the letters entered as he or she types them, which helps catch and eliminate keying errors.

WiViK includes WordQ word prediction and abbreviation. These features help reduce the number of keystrokes needed for typing and can make writing less stressful.

WiViK is also available with a speech-recognition product that may help users with multiple disabilities. Though this product was developed by Bloorview Kids Rehab, it is supported by Prentke Romich.[11]

OnScreen Keyboard

Innovation Management Group's OnScreen keyboard is a highly advanced software package that replaces the need for a physical standard keyboard. It gives access to more than forty-five U.S. and international on-screen keyboards. The software enables verbal confirmation of key inputs and a two to ten times (2x to 10x) Area Magnifier, which will magnify any area of the screen without the need for additional software or hardware. It is equipped with a Word Completion/Prediction program, which offers the user five choices of probable words being entered at a time. Another feature is that the actual on-screen keyboards, buttons, and panels can be set to any of twelve base sizes and can be color coded by the user. This is useful for persons who may have color blindness.

This package is also recommended for libraries that have a large international patron use as it can also be used by patrons who need to use a keyboard with a non-English alphabet display. The software is easy to use, but there is a learning curve as it is complex because it performs a myriad of tasks.[12]

Microsoft and Apple On-Screen Keyboards

Microsoft has incorporated an on-screen keyboard as part of the Windows package since Windows XP. Many professionals acknowledge that versions released with Vista and later are a reliable option for those needing to use an on-screen keyboard.

It is easy to use and supported every step of the way with tutorials.[13] Depending on the version of Microsoft Windows the library owns, the on-screen keyboard will let the user activate it by using menu commands. The directions given are easy to follow, and there is virtually no learning curve. The user can hover over keys, scan the keys, or click on the keys to enter. With Windows 7 there is now a word predictability feature whereby the software predicts the word the user wants at the top of the keyboard. If the word is the one the user wants, he or she simply hovers or clicks on it, and it is entered.

Apple's Mac supports an on-screen keyboard called the Keyboard Viewer, which is found in the Language and Text pane of Systems Preferences. It was designed to float above other applications and can be resized as needed. It works in harmony with other accessibility features, such as Sticky Keys, which empowers the user with increased speed.[14]

Voice-Recognition Technology

Also known as speech recognition, this technology is simultaneously becoming more sophisticated and less costly with each product generation. In 1998, the late Michael Dertouzas, former director of MIT's Laboratory for computer science, and David Arnold, of Olive Tree Software, predicted that "speech will eventually replace the need to use the mouse and keyboard" and probably be used to offer "hands-free access to the computer when driving."[15] Although most users still use keyboards to input information into the computer, some vehicle makers, such as Lexus and Ford, are using the speech-driven commands. Additionally, applications of voice-recognition software are being added to smart phones to enable users to quickly and more efficiently interact with the computer technology.

Voice recognition is a technology that allows a person to use his or her voice as an input device for computer commands. Voice recognition may be used to dictate text, World Wide Web addresses, or commands to the computer (such as saving documents or pulling items off a menu). It is used commercially to route phone calls and handle consumer issues. Although one-word answers such as those used on phone systems do not require training, in general voice recognition uses a neural net to "learn" to recognize a person's voice. As the person speaks, the voice-recognition software remembers the way each word is pronounced. The computer will learn the nuances of the speech patterns by listening to the phonemes and committing them to memory.

This process requires the user to read aloud to the computer an excerpt from one of three passages that will enable the technology to learn the nuances of the speaker's speech patterns. The sounds are presented bit by bit on the computer screen for about thirty minutes. The software accuracy improves as it is used, and much like someone learning a new vocabulary, it may mispronounce words until corrected. The software does not care if the person speaks with an accent, or even clearly, just as long as he or she speaks the same way every time.

Speech recognition is useful for persons who cannot physically use a hardware device to interact with the computer. Additionally, there are groups of educators who find that individuals with learning disabilities are aided by speech-recognition access, as they find the process of dictating words as input is a reliable way to instill students with good oral language skills. The advantage for both groups of users is the same: all that is needed to effectively use computer technology is the ability to speak. What may cause problems, however, is the need for patience in teaching the software speech patterns and the ability to realize when the software is not "hearing" the spoken word correctly.

Training in the use of speech recognition is not a difficult task; it is one, however, that takes some time and patience. A few tips to be successful follow:

1. **Purchase a quality microphone or headset.** Good results are only guaranteed if using a microphone or headset recommended by the software producer. The computer's built-in microphone will not generate acceptable results.
2. **Speak using consistent volume and normal cadence.** If a user's intonation changes during the day—for example, a

person may speak more quickly in the morning than in the
evening—a second computer training session will be necessary and the results saved.

3. **Speak as naturally as possible.** Many people may become
   self-conscious when speaking to the computer and say words
   in unaccustomed ways that they cannot repeat.

4. **Speak clearly and say every part of the word.** There is a tendency for speakers to leave off parts of a word at times. Unless
   it is natural to the speaker to drop off parts of words, say the
   entire word.

5. **Speak at a consistent pace.** Do not speak familiar words faster
   than those being said for the first time.

Dragon Naturally Speaking

Dragon Naturally Speaking is recognized by all as the leader in voice-
recognition systems, and there virtually is no real competition. Dragon Naturally
Speaking helped to pioneer the technology but did not rest on its laurels.
The software will work with virtually all Windows applications, as well as the
Corel product line. Additionally, it works with all e-mails and has recently
been added as an app to mobile phones. The Professional 10 version of Dragon
Naturally Speaking is Section 508 certified and offers hands-free use of the
computer for users with disabilities. The product has a 99 percent accuracy
rate if the user follows the guidelines for use, which are similar to those tips
listed above.

Microsoft's Vista and Windows 7 Release

Microsoft has had some form of speech recognition as part of Windows for
almost a decade, but it hasn't been of the quality as the versions that now
come with Vista and Windows 7. Many professionals acknowledge that
although it is not on par with Dragon Naturally Speaking, the Windows speech-
recognition function will perform well enough to offer the user who needs
a hands-free mode of data entry a good option. The tool is deemed proficient enough for businesses to support its use for standard office procedures
as a way to increase productivity.[16] In fact, mainstream personal computer
professionals offer some really good instructions for using the product,
including the following tips:

1. Ensure that the library's versions of Windows have voice recognition. Go to the control panel menu and type in *Speech*. If the feature is available, a small dialogue box will open, which leads the user to the speech-recognition system. In later versions of Windows, the feature is found in the Ease of Access Center.
2. Print out the instructions, or open a second window for ease in referring to instructions.
3. Ensure that the area around the workstation is as free of ambient noise as possible.
4. Speak at a constant and normal pace; do not exaggerate syllables.
5. When the training is completed, a small toolbar will appear, called the language toolbar. The toolbar is straightforward and uncluttered. It has buttons to turn the microphone on and off; to allow dictation of content; to give voice commands as they relate to Windows applications; to use Speak, which will read content back to the user; and to access Tools, which offers additional settings.

The training session should be saved to enable the patron to use it the next time he or she visits the library. If library policy does not permit the saving of this type of data, the patron will have to train the computer each time it is used.

Apple's Mac System

Apple's Mac system enables users to navigate menus, enter keyboard shortcuts, open and close applications, and so forth, using a tool called Speakable Items. It is not necessary to train the Mac to learn the user's voice to use this utility. Speakable Items will not enable the use of speech dictation for any other application.

The Right Furniture

One extremely important and basic need is purchasing furniture designed for persons with physical disabilities. Keep in mind that the patron using a wheelchair to navigate the library and access the computer should be able to "wheel" himself or herself under the table on which the computer rests; select furniture that will allow this (adjustable-height tables allow for different-sized wheelchairs and users).

Ensure that the computer monitor is at a comfortable viewing height; persons in wheelchairs spend a lot of their time looking up, and anything that can be done to alleviate this is useful. If purchasing new workstation equipment, consider adding a monitor arm, which will allow the user to place the monitor where needed. A keyboard tray will ensure that the work surface is not cluttered and that the keyboard is ergonomically placed.

It is important to have good task lighting available in the workstation area. This feature is often overlooked, as we are dependent on overhead lighting. Task lighting focuses light where it is needed and helps users see where USB connections actually connect.

Choose a sturdy, well-balanced chair that will not roll or tip for the workstation seating. If a person using a wheelchair will be using the workstation for a long period of time, he or she may wish to transfer to another chair and needs assurance that the transfer will be a safe one. A chair with arms (although not standard in a computer workstation) and four legs is a wise choice for people using walkers or canes, for it presents a stable base to transfer their weight. See figure 7.5 for an example of a Steelcase workstation that meets many of these criteria.

Start at the Beginning

Architectural accessibility is as important as technical accessibility. Choosing the right furniture and locating the workstation in an accessible location are the logical first steps. It is easiest to develop two workstations for assistive technologies. One would be for persons with visual and learning disabilities and the other for those with some physical disabilities or cognitive disabilities or those who need to use different means of inputting information beyond the standard keyboard or mouse.

It bears repeating to suggest that libraries should work with their advisory group and local agencies who work with and for people with disabilities. Often groups may have excess hardware that they are willing to give to nonprofit agencies like the library. These groups might even be able to provide consultants and staff training free of charge.

The library should use the products it has on hand (e.g., Microsoft's products), then start to purchase items that will do the most good for the widest

Figure 7.5
Well-Designed, Accessible Furniture Arrangement

A well-designed computer station, which includes an adjustable worktable, assistive technologies, task lighting, and comfortable and safe seating, enables persons with disabilities to independently access information.

audience. For example, although the Senior Mouse is a specialized mouse, it is actually a good example of a product that can be deemed a universal design product. It can be used by the entire population, and people are not hindered by having to use it. The library can purchase these for the accessible workstation and gradually replace them at all workstations.

Build a treasure chest of input devices one device at a time if necessary. Some are low priced enough to ask Friends of the Library to sponsor them. The library gains access for its patrons, and the Friends know they've made a tangible difference to the library's ability to serve the entire population.

Notes

1. An overview of Microsoft's available Accessibility tools can be found at www .microsoft.com/enable/.
2. Both Microsoft and Apple support a variety of keyboard shortcuts that enable users with dexterity or mobility problems (or both) to input data with greater

ease. Visit http://windows.microsoft.com/en-us/windows-vista/Using
-keyboard-shortcuts and www.apple.com/accessibility/macosx/physical.html.

3. A mouthstick is used by patrons who have determined that this is their most reliable method of inputting data. Patrons place one end of their personal stick in their mouth and use the other end to tap the keys.

4. To get a better picture of the IntelliKeys product and to determine if it is a viable product for the library, see the Assistive Technology Training Online Project's IntelliKeys Tutorial at http://atto.buffalo.edu/registered/Tutorials/intellikeys/index.php.

5. The Senior Mouse allows the user to fully extend his or her hand over the device. For a list of vendors, visit www.incap-at.de/index.php?article_id =1&clang=1.

6. In addition to developing specialized products like the Zero Pressure Finger Mouse, Special Needs Computer Solutions has a large inventory of products for people with disabilities and different access needs. Their website is logical and well organized: www.specialneedscomputers.ca/index.php?l=product _detail&p=589.

7. Cirque Corporation offers both mainstream as well as special use touch pads. Further information about these items can be found at www.cirque.com.

8. Although the product is available from a number of mainstream vendors, additional information can be found at the AbleNet website: www.ablenetinc.com.

9. The AbleLink Technologies website (www.ablelinktech.com) offers a good overview of how its products can help individuals with cognitive disabilities. Although the library may not purchase these items, an awareness of available products is useful.

10. TrackerPro, available from Madentec, enables persons who can move only their heads to effectively use computers. The sensor is mounted to the computer screen, and the user places a reflective dot on a part of his or her eye glasses or forehead. As the user moves his or her head, the tracker will follow and move the cursor. This is not meant for traditional gaming. For a more thorough overview of this product, visit the Madentec website, at www .madentec.com/products/tracker-pro.php.

11. WiViK offers a full range of on-screen keyboards; for an overview or to download a trial copy of the product, visit the WiViK website, at www.wivik.com/description.html.

12. To download a trial copy of the software, visit the Innovation Management Group website, at www.imgpresents.com/onscreen/onsdemo.htm#download.

13. The Microsoft Accessibility tutorials can be found at www.microsoft.com/enable/training/.

14. Further information on Apple's onscreen keyboard can be found on the Apple Mac Accessibility Physical and Motor Skills On-Screen Keyboard web page, at www.apple.com/accessibility/macosx/physical.html.
15. Brad Stone, "Are You Talking to Me?" *Newsweek,* March 2, 1998, 85–86.
16. See ProductivityPortfolio's "Using Voice Recognition to Power Microsoft Word," at www.timeatlas.com/useful_utilities/free/use_your_voice_to_power _microsoft_word; and Adam Pash, "Control Your PC with Your Voice," *Lifehacker,* http://lifehacker.com/391884/control-your-pc-with-your-voice.

8
Accessible Collections, Resources, and Discussion Forums

The availability of information in electronic format is exploding, and as it does, people with disabilities needing information in an accessible format are also finding their ability to locate information increasing. Basically, if the text is stored digitally and correctly tagged, it can be converted to a usable format by people who cannot use traditional print. This trend presents libraries with the opportunity to become a bridge to these resources for people with variable text requirements. They can do this by being aware of the free information that is accessible and linking to it, purchasing and circulating unique electronic texts used by families with special needs, subscribing to the fee-based resources that are accessible, and advocating for accessibility when databases are not usable by all patrons. Virtual meeting spaces allow readers who can't physically visit the library the opportunity to participate in library programs. The resources and devices highlighted in this chapter will be valuable aids to persons requiring assistive technology.

Digital Information Resources

National Library Service for the Blind and Physically Handicapped (NLS)

The National Library Service for the Blind and Physically Handicapped (NLS), a division of the Library of Congress, works with cooperating library agencies to bring specially formatted books, magazines, musical scores, and more to eligible citizens at home and abroad free of charge.[1] Patrons may borrow audiobooks or Braille books and magazines similar to those found in their local public library.

The National Library Service is in the process of migrating from an analog platform to a digital format. In addition to providing listeners a cleaner and clearer sound, the digital format will also extend instant access to the NLS

Figure 8.1
NLS Digital Book and Cartridge

Working with consumers, engineers, and librarians, the National Library Service for the Blind and Physically Handicapped developed a quality, usable, and accessible playback system for patrons of the library.

collection for patrons with an e-mail account and registered with the NLS program. The NLS program is operating digital service in two modes: hardware based and web based. The former is more traditional and uses books that have been loaded onto flash drives and are in cartridge form to be mailed through the U.S. Postal Service to readers at a defined mailing address. Figure 8.1 shows the hardware components. Readers need to use a specially provided digital player to listen to the recordings, as copyright law requires that only patrons eligible for the service may receive them.

The other mode allows patrons to download similar materials from a secure website and is part of the Braille and Audio Reading Download (BARD) project.

NLS Braille and Audio Reading Download (BARD) Project

The NLS Braille and Audio Reading Download (BARD) project is the second option of the digital program. BARD allows eligible patrons to download available titles from the NLS database to their computers, players, or onto a flash drive. This gives patrons instant access to titles they previously may have had to wait months to receive. Patrons signing up for the service are given a password that will give them access to the NLS catalog. They then follow a set of simple instructions, and the book is delivered to the computer. If patrons do not have access to a computer and the library policy allows, staff can assist patrons with downloading and transferring the book to a flash drive, which the patron can use with their playback machine.

Canadian National Institute for the Blind (CNIB) Library

The Canadian National Institute for the Blind (CNIB) Library is recognized as one of the most innovative providers of digital technologies for persons with special reading needs. In addition to providing books in digital format, the CNIB maintains a children's porthole, which enables registered youth across Canada to chat. The CNIB partners with public libraries to enable patrons to have services where they live. The collection of books, magazines, and newspapers are broad ranged and some are bilingual.[2]

Commercial Players

Some patrons may also opt to purchase a smaller, more portable player to play titles they borrow from the libraries and that also have been encrypted to ensure only eligible users can avail themselves of the service.[3] Should the library have funds to purchase these devices for loan to individuals considering purchasing them, patrons will be able to "try before they buy." Figure 8.2 below illustrates two products currently in the marketplace. They are available from GW Micro (Booksense) and HumanWare (Victor Reader Stream). These companies only provide the hardware and do not provide content.

Bookshare

Bookshare, www.bookshare.org, is a web-based nonprofit organization that maintains a digital library of books that volunteer members have scanned and proofread, making the information available for other eligible patrons to convert to large print, Braille, or synthetic speech, with the proviso that only eligible patrons can access the database. All patrons of Bookshare must be certified as eligible to receive the service. The eligibility guidelines are

Figure 8.2
Digital Players

Patrons who wish more portability in their listening experience may opt to purchase a commercial proprietary digital player such as these available from GW Micro and HumanWare.

the same as those of the National Library Service. Although the majority of the works are volunteer produced, some publishers are contributing texts directly to the organization.

The Bookshare library provides people with print disabilities in the United States legal access to more than 50,000 books and 150 periodicals. These books include best sellers, school texts, and royalty-free titles. Bookshare is a subscription-based service operated by Benetech Initiative. There is a nominal registration fee and an annual membership fee to use Bookshare although all students are exempt from the fee, including adult-education students.

The library offers two complimentary e-book readers that read text into synthetic speech, and it points users to a commercial product, Read:OutLoud, an e-book reader that will also work with its books.[4]

Recording for the Blind and Dyslexic (RFB&D)

Recording for the Blind and Dyslexic (RFB&D) was founded on the belief that "education is a right, not a privilege."[5] RFB&D supports a network of volunteers and professionals dedicated to providing educational texts to eligible students of all ages who cannot use standard print materials. Eligibility requirements are the same as those for the NLS, but there is a nominal enrollment fee and annual subscription fee requirement to use the resources.

The library of holdings is vast, circulating more than 500,000 books a year. It includes titles that have been recorded and formatted digitally for easy access by users. Like the titles available through the NLS program, specialized software or hardware is needed to listen to the materials. Members of RFB&D may opt to borrow a physical copy of the title or download it to their playback unit through the AudioAccess option. RFB&D's books will work with a variety of conventional playback devices.

OverDrive

OverDrive is a commercial information provider and maintains OverDrive Digital Library Reserve. The company provides libraries with popular audiobooks, e-books, music, and videos to lend to patrons for download. Although there are similar electronic collection providers, OverDrive is committed to offering an accessible book collection and works with libraries to ensure that patrons using screen readers and enlargers can access these materials.

Staff of this company have worked extensively with patrons, accessibility providers, and knowledgeable librarians to develop easy-to-follow instructions, and they have developed access to keyboard shortcuts that OverDrive customers can link to.[6] OverDrive's platform supports JAWS and Window-Eyes screen readers.

Additionally, OverDrive is the exclusive provider of digital content, management, and storage for the National Instructional Materials Access Center. This translates into 19,000 core curriculum titles from eighty-six publishers that can be formatted into accessible Braille, audio, or large-print versions of the original text.

The Kindle

For readers who are visually impaired or have a learning disability, Amazon's Kindle current reader has afforded them a format for reading new books and magazines that simulates the reading experience. The Kindle allows those with limited sight to supersize the font display using seven large fonts. Keep in mind, however, the viewing area for the text display is limited; therefore, the enlarging possibilities are likewise limited.

The text-to-speech feature that comes with the Kindle DX has undergone litigation in the publishers' rights arena as well as on behalf of persons with visual disabilities. Although authors recognized that those with disabilities should have access, they were concerned about their livelihood by ceding potential audio rights to the titles. People with disabilities wanted the ability to purchase the titles when they were released.

Some of this discussion was moot, however, because although the Kindle was independently usable by those with low vision or who had a learning disability, those who were blind could not use the menu, as it was inaccessible. The authors settled with Amazon by agreeing that their books would not be released audibly for three months after general release. Consumer groups such as the National Federation of the Blind successfully lobbied Amazon to include an audible menu system. New versions of the Kindle will come "equipped with a voice guide that reads all menu options aloud so blind and other print-disabled people can navigate the device menus."[7]

Some people who have developed diminished vision later in life say reading with the Kindle enables them to read as they did when their vision allowed them to read standard print books. Some are rebuilding libraries that they had in print in electronic format. Additionally, the Kindle is physically lightweight and may actually be more accessible to persons who cannot hold a heavy book. The page-turning attribute in the Kindle may also be more accessible to persons who cannot physically turn a page in conventional books.

The Sony Reader

The Sony Reader is a digital book reader, currently available in the United States, Canada, and Europe. It not only stores hundreds of books on a single electronic device but also enables readers with low vision to adjust the size of the text on the screen according to their needs. The Sony Reader supports five font sizes, but some users with low vision feel that the display is clearer and easier to read, albeit smaller, than that of competitors' products. Users with low vision have the ability to download titles from a variety of sources and can create libraries of accessible titles that are retrievable on demand. The Sony Style website offers an overview of the products and purchasing information.[8]

ReadHowYouWant—Special Format on Demand

ReadHowYouWant is a relatively young, Australia-based company that successfully developed conversion technology that reformats existing books into high-quality alternative formats quickly, easily, and at a price comparable to standard format books. The company has partnerships with publishers throughout the world, which allows them to convert works to large-print, audible, e-format (all formats supported), or Braille format. Should students or patrons need titles not available in special formats, and budgets allow, ReadHowYouWant can produce the book for the library.

Also worth noting, ReadHowYouWant can also publish the library's organizational materials in accessible formats.[9] Staff at this company are well versed in formatting needs and will produce professional-looking documents.

Playaways

Playaways are a patented format of audible books in the MP3 format, produced by Findaway World. This company has partnerships with many producers of recorded books to download and sell their titles in this format. The thousands of titles available in the library reflect the reading needs of the general public.

The devices are lightweight and portable and remember where the users stopped reading and will return to the spot when they wish to start listening again. The feature that makes them accessible to people who are visually impaired, blind, or learning disabled is the logical layout of the function keys. A brief orientation of the keys by a sighted user very often is all that is needed for the user to access current titles without needing access to specialized playback equipment.

There are a few issues concerning Playaways that could be problematic in the general library environment. Because the unit runs on batteries, it will not be usable unless batteries are included. Staff should ensure that batteries are in the unit and functioning before circulation or alert readers that they are not included. Another issue is that they do require an output mode to be heard (i.e., devices such as headphones, earbuds, or speakers). Although Playaways come with a set of earbuds, the library should not feel obligated to provide them. An initial set can be given to patrons who cannot afford to purchase them or sold to those who can.

Findaway World is committed to enabling its product to be used by as many people as possible and seeks user input on ways to make products more usable. The Playaway website incorporates use instructions for people who are blind or have low vision.[10] Figure 8.3 shows the current Playaway product.

Using Cyber Meeting Spaces

Libraries offer patrons more than information; they also offer entertaining and enriching programs. People with disabilities often find it difficult to attend these events, as transportation may be difficult to arrange. Online meeting rooms, which are accessible to the widest population, allow the library's community to come together to discuss books, listen to authors, and learn more about the library regardless of where the patrons live or what type of ability or disability they possess. They enable lunchtime book discussions from patron's offices, dorm rooms, or kitchens. All of these meeting rooms are not accessible.

Online Programming for All Libraries (OPAL) Talking Communities Online Meeting Rooms

Talking Communities is a software company used by Online Programming for All Libraries (OPAL) that allows the greatest cross section of the people

Figure 8.3
Playaway Device

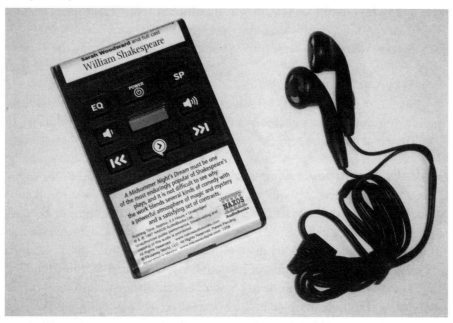

The general consumer Playaway technology is accessible to persons with visual disabilities because of the logical layout of the function buttons.

to speak or type their comments. OPAL provides a low-cost method for libraries to open a meeting space online, as costs are shared among members. The technology is simple to learn and offers users the opportunity to either speak their thoughts or type their thoughts. For groups that may have individuals who are blind or deaf in the same meeting at the same time, some interpretation may be necessary. Basically, after installing an applet onto a computer, the patron can participate in either of two ways:

Via text chat. The user with vision and wishing to type his or her information would move the cursor into the text chat input box located in the left center area of the screen. Once there, the patron would type the message and press the Return or Enter key on the keyboard. The message is displayed in the text chat display block for all in the meeting room to see.

Via Voiceover IP. Patrons who wish to speak to participate would press and hold the Ctrl key when it is their turn to speak and be heard by everyone in the online room. When users have finished speaking, they release the Ctrl key. The software monitors whose turn it is to speak and maintains the order.

A useful feature of OPAL, which makes it a true library, is that past programs are stored and can be accessed at will. Libraries can select the size of room they need and can afford.[11]

Serotek Corporation's Accessible Events

If the library occasionally hosts events that may be of interest to persons who physically cannot visit the library, consider subscribing to Serotek Corporation's Accessible Event online meeting resource. The Accessible Event works by providing attendees with the website address, event number, and a log-in code. Applets do not have to be downloaded on the attendees' side. The site is accessible for users who are blind, deaf, and deaf-blind. Attendees can fully participate in the event either by hearing the speaker and any printed documents that may be presented or by viewing with captioning. There are options for subscribing to one session or a yearly subscription.[12]

Creating a Usable Electronic Links Library

It is useful to collect and build an electronic links library, which will enable persons with disabilities, their families, their friends, and their instructors to quickly link to resources that are accessible as well as helpful. The resources can be suggestions made by patrons, consumer groups, and collection development specialists. In addition to offering a link to the NLS program, the following resources will get staff started:

Accessible Books. www.setbc.org/setbc/accessiblebooks/free booksforyou.html. This collection of books was compiled by the Special Education Technology Division in British Columbia, Canada. Unlike other electronic libraries, many of these are picture books that illustrate concepts or seek to instruct the reader to perform a specific task.

American Sign Language Browser. http://commtechlab.msu.edu/ sites/aslweb/browser.htm. The Communication Technology Laboratory at Michigan State University supports a library of videos demonstrating words in American Sign Language. The site also links to other resources of interest to persons needing information on communicating with persons who are deaf as well as deaf-blind.

Classic Reader. http://ClassicReader.com, and *Project Gutenberg,* www.gutenberg.org. The library can extend its classics collection in electronic media by pointing readers to Classic Reader and Project Gutenberg. The collections found on these websites extend to titles whose copyright protection has expired. The Classic Reader library contains works by still-in-demand authors, such as Zane Grey, Mary Roberts Rinehart, and Agatha Christie. There are also books on the children's reading level, including series such as the Bobbsey Twins and Eleanor H. Porter's titles, which some older adults enjoy revisiting. Classic Reader also provides a links library to other resources, such as the Online Medieval and Classical Library and the Christian Classic Ethereal Library, both of which contain works not found elsewhere electronically.

Folktexts. www.pitt.edu/~dash/folktexts.html. A text-based collection of folktales, fairy tales, and myths.

Lit2Go. http://etc.usf.edu/lit2go/. A collection of stories and poems, in MP3 format, which can be downloaded to personal players, read on the computer, or printed.

NIH SeniorHealth. http://nihseniorhealth.gov/index.html. In addition to having up-to-date and useful information on health issues, the National Institutes of Health SeniorHealth website is one of the best designed. Each page allows the user to increase or decrease text size, adjust contrast, or open a screen reader. All videos provide text alternatives.

UDL Book Builder. http://bookbuilder.cast.org. This website allows visitors to create, share, publish, and read digital books, according to their unique needs and abilities.

UDL Editions. http://udleditions.cast.org. UDL Editions is an interactive collection of books that seeks to reach and engage all learners ages ten and up. Vocabulary is built through pictures and definitions.

Voice Thread. http://voicethread.com/?#home. Voice Thread is a platform that enables conversations to occur by speech, picture, text, webcam, or MP3 format. This would be a unique tool to use for reading clubs, as it offers the ability to take programs out of the physical library to patrons who may not physically be able to visit the library.

Zac Browser. www.zacbrowser.org. Developed for children living with variants of autism spectrum disorder, the Zac Browser takes over the controls for the user, removing many of the distractions that prevent the Internet from being used effectively. Zac will only enable visits to sites it deems usable and acceptable for children with this disability. Utilities are included, such as a drawing board, which is useful to persons with autism.

Resources for Patrons with Autism or Cognitive Disabilities

Some people with autism, as well as those with cognitive disabilities, can learn through interactions with computers and software. Titles available in CD format address issues such as birthdays, geography, community relations, facial recognition, and more. The titles are not inexpensive and are sometimes out of reach for families who need them the most.

Still other families use storyboards to communicate with members who have autism or speech or language disorders. The basic board itself is pricey, and each additional teaching unit requires a separate purchase. For example, Mayer-Johnson makes the Boardmaker, which enables teachers to print symbols and pictures to communicate daily life needs. But some units, such as "Print 'n Learn Community Units," explain community mainstays such as school, mall, restaurant, firehouse, and post office. Or "Cooking Up Fun" enables students to learn about daily activities such as shopping, cooking, eating, cleaning up, and reading recipes.[13]

Visiting some sites that promote educational opportunities for people with these disabilities, or asking professionals who work with people who have these disabilities, can help the library create a lending library of titles.[14]

Build an Accessible Library Collection and They Will Come

The library can start to build an accessible electronic library collection for its website by simply being aware of what makes a site accessible. Be sure that as staff members build the links library, they present the links in an accessible format.

Although it is important to provide readers with electronic information, it is also important to remember that there is still demand for books on CD and in large print. If the library can only afford to purchase one format of a title, why not purchase it in large print? It extends the usability of the book.[15] Likewise, DVDs are being formatted with audio descriptions and closed-captioning. Be sure that the library purchases editions that contain these accessibility features, as some vendors are providing stripped-down versions of the titles. The library's collection development funds should be used to purchase materials the entire community can use whenever possible.

Notes

1. Eligibility requirements as well as links to the network of cooperating library agencies may be found at www.loc.gov/nls/what.html.
2. To learn more about the CNIB, visit the website and listen to or view a very informative video about the service that the CNIB produced for their patrons: www.cnib.ca/en/services/library/.
3. HumanWare, www.humanware.com, manufactures the Victor Reader Stream, and GW Micro, www.gwmicro.com, manufactures Booksense. Both are small (four to eight ounces) and easy to use and offer readers the discretion of carrying the devices in pockets, purses, backpacks, and so forth. Both products support NLS downloads as well as those from commercial and other nonprofit entities.
4. The Read:OutLoud e-book reader is available from Don Johnston at www .donjohnston.com.
5. To become a member or to learn more about RFB&D, visit the website, at www .rfbd.org/about.htm.
6. To learn more about OverDrive's accessibility efforts, see www.overdrive.com/ software/omc/accessibility.asp.
7. PR Newswire, "National Federation of the Blind Commends Amazon on New Availing of Accessible Kindle," July 29, 2010, www.prnewswire.com/ news-releases/national-federation-of-the-blind-commends-amazon-on -unveiling-of-new-accessible-kindle-99555314.html.
8. To learn more about the Sony Reader, visit the Sony Style website, at www .sonystyle.com.

9. To learn more about ReadHowYouWant, visit www.readhowyouwant.com.

10. To learn more about Playaway's policies concerning libraries, and to see the titles available to libraries, visit www.playawaylibrary.com/index.cfm.

11. Libraries wishing to learn more about OPAL, or to peruse programs held by OPAL libraries, may visit www.opal-online.org. Subscription information may also be obtained there.

12. Accessible Event is a subsidiary of Serotek Corporation. To learn more or sit in on a mock accessible event, visit http://accessibleevent.com.

13. Boardmaker (available from Mayer-Johnson, at www.mayer-johnson.com) is excellent, as there are many individual titles that are useful to families to learn communication, daily living, and coping skills.

14. The book *My School Day,* available from www.autismcoach.com, is one example of a title that, once used and absorbed, is no longer needed in a household and is better borrowed from a library. Consider using Closing the Gap's resource library to build a collection and make connections. Although a low-cost membership fee is required, the organization does offer trial memberships; further information may be found at www.closingthegap.com. Also, do not hesitate to ask parents of children with autism what they would like to borrow. Assure parents that if they donate titles they no longer use to the library, the books will be recirculated to other patrons.

15. Large-print-resources publishers typically publish books in 16- to 18-point type. A listing of the publishers may be found at www.loc.gov/nls/reference/circulars/largeprint.html.

9
Staff Make It All Work

Library administrators and assistive-technology staff may assemble the most accessible website and workstation for persons with disabilities, but it will be for naught if the Human Resources Department is not working on a staff training module to ensure that people with disabilities are treated in a professional and knowledgeable manner. If the library environment does not provide the support the person with a disability needs, he or she will not return.

Although our culture is making some progress in seeing people with disabilities as people first, stereotypes still prevail. Ensuring that all staff members have an awareness of the types of disabilities patrons may have and the access solutions the library owns should be a primary goal for the library. This directive includes staff who may be providing remote reference services or handling help lines. All staff should be given an overview of all the technology the library owns as part of their in-service training.

The ALA's Association of Specialized and Cooperative Library Agencies (ASCLA) maintains a tool kit entitled "Library Accessibility: What You Need to Know." The tool kit's tip sheets are useful and educational, and they address most disabilities and audiences. They can be downloaded and reproduced free of charge.[1] It is recommended that these tip sheets be shared with appropriate staff and trustees and periodically discussed during staff development opportunities.

Staff should be comfortable when working with people with disabilities because a person who is blind can sense negative body language, and people who are deaf can hear the sighs by looking at frowns; therefore, take the time to instruct and remind staff that quality service applies to the entire population.

"People First" Language and Attitude

Staff members need to realize that people with disabilities are individuals; no two may share the exact same dreams, goals, or desires. They should be aware, however, that some may share the same dreams, goals, and desires they do. People with disabilities may not take the same steps to reach goals, or it may take longer to take the steps, but determination and access to education and information can be the means by which they can reach like goals.

People with disabilities share humanity's gifts of laughter and tears, pleasure and sorrow, and the ups and downs of daily living. People with disabilities can be nice, people with disabilities can be nasty, people with disabilities can be polite, and people with disabilities can be rude; people with disabilities can be young, people with disabilities can be old; people with disabilities come in all shapes, sizes, and races. It is important to remember this mantra: "People with disabilities are people first," and they should be treated accordingly. Table 9.1 brings the point across that words and language matter, and positive words can empower people.[2]

Basic Etiquette

When working with patrons in general, the most basic rule is, of course, the Golden Rule—treat patrons as you would want to be treated. This extends to people with disabilities as well. There are two major mistakes one can make when a person with a disability comes into the service area: one is to send out an alarm (e.g., announcing to coworkers that there is a "blind man in the library"); the second mistake is to ignore the person when he or she enters the library. Although common sense should be everyone's guideline, it's realistic to say that not all persons are endowed with the same degree of common sense; thus, guidelines are offered. They are offered with the advisory that each person is unique and may need different tools and assistance. Here are some general rules to follow:

Table 9.1
"People First" Terms: Using the terminology in this table will let persons with disabilities know that the library always sees them as people first

Affirmative Phrases	Negative Phrases
person with an intellectual, cognitive, or developmental disability	retarded; mentally defective
person who is blind; person who is visually impaired	the blind
person with a disability	the disabled; handicapped
person who is deaf	the deaf; deaf and dumb
person who is hard-of-hearing	suffers a hearing loss
person who has multiple sclerosis	afflicted by MS
person with cerebral palsy	CP victim
person with epilepsy; person with seizure disorder	epileptic
person who uses a wheelchair	confined or restricted to a wheelchair
person who has muscular dystrophy	stricken by MD
person with a physical disability; physically disabled	crippled; lame; deformed
unable to speak; uses synthetic speech	dumb; mute
person with psychiatric disability	crazy; nuts
person who is successful; productive	has overcome his/her disability; is courageous (when it implies the person has courage because of having a disability)

1. Be natural when working with a person with a disability; do not compensate (e.g., do not add a cloyingly sweet or sympathetic tone to your speech pattern).
2. Talk directly to the person with a disability unless it is impossible.
3. Offer your assistance rather than assisting.
4. When unsure of how to proceed in a situation, ask the person for advice.

5. Do not estrange persons with disabilities from the general patron population.

6. Remember, there are invisible differences, such as hearing or cognitive impairments, that might necessitate that you repeat the question using different words.

7. Be patient. Although this is often the hardest thing to do on a stressful day, it is important. Refer to the person's disability only if it is relevant to the conversation.

8. Use correct language concerning disabilities whenever possible. If you make a mistake, relax and try not to repeat it.

9. Treat adults with disabilities as adults (even if their intellectual level may be of a lesser level) and children with disabilities as children.

Special Considerations When Assisting Persons with Low Vision or Blindness

It is important to realize that 75 percent of the population who are legally blind are not totally blind and have some vision. Some people may use a white cane or a guide dog. Some people with low vision may be able to travel safely and effectively without a cane, and staff may not be aware that they have a visual impairment that may require assistance. Staff cannot be faulted if they do not offer special assistance in cases such as these; however, the general environment should be one in which patrons feel comfortable enough to request help when needed.

Even though each person and each disability will be dealt with on a one-to-one basis, there are general guidelines that should always be followed when working with persons who have a visual impairment.[3]

1. If you are working with someone who is blind or visually impaired, identify yourself when you first meet him or her and orientate the person to the surroundings.

2. When orientating the person to the library environment, use specific directions. If the person is to follow a path to the washroom, for instance, say, "Walk about five feet, then turn left, and it's two feet on your left."

3. Keep your voice natural and conversational while being an active listener. Give audible cues to let the person know you

are still listening. Alert him or her when you are leaving the conversation area.

4. Ask the patron if he or she needs assistance navigating to his or her destination within the library. If so, offer your crooked arm, allowing the patron to hold your arm slightly above the elbow. Walk naturally, and be mindful of narrow passages and doorways.

5. If offering a person a chair, ensure that he or she knows where the chair back is as well as the seat.

6. When orientating new users on the computer, it is necessary to be specific. For example, function keys are sometimes in different locations on keyboards, so explain that on the library's keyboard, for example, the Delete key is the key at the farthest corner of the keyboard.

7. Never pet a guide dog or give it food. Staff may inform the patron where the dog may relieve itself and where water for the dog may be located.

Special Considerations When Assisting Persons with Hearing Impairments or Deafness

Many times people who are deaf will visit the library without anyone being aware that they have a disability unless they need to have an oral conversation. There are times when staff may feel that someone just isn't listening or paying attention to what is being said, when in reality the person cannot hear what is being said.

The degree of hearing impairment and the individual's own ability to interact in a hearing environment will determine what special services are needed. If the library owns personal communication devices for persons who are hearing impaired, ensure that both staff and patrons know they are available. Be aware that the library's security devices, which emit sound, may cause problems for persons using hearing aids. Following are some basic tips that can be used when interacting with persons who are hearing impaired.[4]

1. People who are deaf use a variety of ways to communicate, such as lipreading, sign language, speaking, and writing. Ask the patron how he or she wishes to converse. Be aware

that all techniques require eye contact to be successful, so be careful not to turn your face away while speaking.

2. Seek a quiet environment for conversation. Be mindful that there is not a bright light source behind you as that will make it more difficult for the person to see your face. Ensure the patron that it is OK for him or her to speak loudly. Some patrons with hearing difficulties are hesitant to speak in libraries as they have been taught that libraries are quiet places.

3. Be sure you have the person's attention before you start to speak. You can wave your hand, touch a person's shoulder, or tap on the table.

4. Do not have objects in your mouth, like gum or candy, and keep your hands away from your face when you are speaking to the patron.

5. State the topic of the conversation, and if the topic of the conversation changes, be sure the patron realizes a new subject is being discussed.

6. Speak clearly and at a moderate pace, pausing between sentences, and allow the patron to view your facial expressions.

7. Do not shout. Shouting makes the speaker look angry and actually distorts the sound signal.

8. Be prepared to rephrase words if there is a communication problem. For example, if a patron's fine is fifty cents and he or she hears fifteen cents, staff can try saying it as half a dollar or simply write the amount out on a slip of paper.

9. If a long conversation is foreseen, and oral communication is not working sufficiently, move to a computer with a word processor and type the conversation.

10. Always talk directly to the patron who is deaf while being patient, positive, and natural.

Special Considerations When Assisting Persons with Mobility Impairments

United Cerebral Palsy's definition of mobility impairment is easy to understand and is the one used for this discussion. It is "the inability of a person to use one or more of his/her extremities or a lack of strength to walk, grasp, or lift objects. The use of a wheelchair, crutches, or a walker may be utilized to aid in mobility."[5] People may have mobility impairments because of diseases, such as arthritis; neurological (brain) disorders, such as cerebral palsy; or neuromuscular diseases, such as muscular dystrophy. They may have a mobility impairment as a result of an accident or a disease that necessitated the amputation of limbs or rendered them paraplegic or quadriplegic. The needs of people with mobility impairments are diverse; however, the following tips are offered when working with persons with mobility impairments.[6]

1. If the person is using a wheelchair or scooter, do not assume you may purposely touch the devices. These mobility aides, in a manner of speaking, are acting as a person's "legs" and are part of his or her personal space.
2. Speak directly to the person in the wheelchair, not the person who may be pushing the wheelchair. If you see that the conversation is going to be a long one, position yourself and the patron in a space where you can sit and be at eye level with the patron.
3. Staff should be aware of which of the library's furnishings will accommodate wheelchairs or scooters. Be sure chairs offered to patrons will allow them to support themselves as they transfer from a wheeled vehicle.
4. When directing people, think about the easiest way to get somewhere, not the shortest. Staff should ensure that pathways are clutter-free.
5. Staff should offer patrons using canes or walkers a "rest stop" if guiding them to resources that are at a distance.
6. In program situations where there are a lot of people in attendance, ensure that there are adequate staff members available to assist people should an emergency evacuation be necessary.

Special Considerations When Assisting Persons with Learning Disabilities

People with learning disabilities will not appear to be any different than those persons without this disability. They simply process information differently and need to learn differently. More than likely, they will have to identify themselves as having a learning disability and needing special assistance.

There are a myriad of defined learning disabilities that affect people, including dyslexia, dyscalculia, auditory and visual processing disorders, and nonverbal learning disorders. The type of learning disability the person has as well as his or her intellectual ability will dictate the accommodations the person will need. Generally, however, following these basic tips will result in a positive interaction.[7]

1. Do not speak quickly but use clear articulation and pause after finishing a thought to ensure the patron comprehends it.
2. Be precise in word choice. If the patron does not understand what is being said, reword statements rather than repeating.
3. Simultaneously combine verbal and visual information. For example, rather than telling the patron to fill out an application, hand him or her the application, pointing out spaces that need to be filled in.
4. Some patrons may not be able to independently read printed instructions and will need them read aloud.
5. Some learning disabilities cause individuals to become easily distracted. You may need to bring them back into the conversation by alerting them that they have drifted.
6. Try to eliminate all outside distractions by conducting the instructions or conversations in less traveled and quieter areas of the library. Offer headphones to patrons who need to study or use a computer if the library is particularly noisy.
7. When offering readers' advisory service, do not presume to know at what reading level the patrons are capable. Ask them to share a title they recently enjoyed and offer titles on that reading level.

Special Considerations When Assisting Persons with Autism Spectrum Disorders (ASDs)

One of the most complex and varied disabilities patrons might have who visit the library is an autism spectrum disorder (ASD). People who have ASDs may have impairments in language, social skills, and sensory integration and processing. In the library setting, these persons may not demonstrate ASD-related behaviors until interacting with staff.[8]

A patron with ASD may not be verbal or may talk in the third person, or the patron may talk *at* you rather than converse. They may not understand jokes or idioms. They often lack the ability to read body language and take social cues or be aware of what is acceptable library behavior. Some people may be sensitive to loud noises, bright lights, or odors such as cleaners or perfumes. People with ASDs communicate differently using verbal communication, sign language, communication boards, and written words. Communication will have to be conducted to the patron's mode.

Library visits should always be a positive experience both for the patrons and the staff. The following are some general tips for working with individuals with autism spectrum disorders.[9]

1. If the patron comes with a caregiver, communicate directly with the patron, not the caregiver unless, of course, the patron does not want to talk with you.
2. Keep language simple and concrete. Do not use figurative statements, such as "See you later," as the person might expect to see you later. Whenever possible, do not offer multiple choices.
3. Do not insist on social norms such as having someone look at you when you are conversing even if it is only the two of you at the computer station.
4. Be predictable and specific; tell the patron what you are doing and when you are going to do it—the term *later* doesn't suffice. It's better to say, "I am going to begin the computer lesson at 2:00 p.m." rather than say, "The computer lesson will be starting soon."
5. Converse visually if your points are not being understood. Use pictures or online whiteboard technology to communicate.
6. When providing instructions, avoid lengthy verbal instructions, and break tasks down to clearly defined steps.
7. Stick to a routine that the patrons are comfortable with. If they come into the library to return a book, then use the washroom, and then look for another book, do not insist that they

look at a book you've selected for them before going to the washroom.

8. Staff should be aware of where people are in case of the need for an emergency evacuation. Flashing lights and loud noises may cause them great stress.

Special Considerations When Assisting Persons with Cognitive Differences

Patrons with developmental disabilities or cognitive disabilities (or both) have limitations in mental functioning and may need more time to learn new tasks and process information. Contrary to stereotypes—which depict all people with cognitive differences to be like the character Forrest Gump or look like a person with Down syndrome—they are not likely to have any distinguishable physical characteristics.

Although some people are born with cognitive disabilities, some develop them. This may be caused by the aging process, because when some people age, their cognitive abilities diminish and the ability to solve problems quickly becomes impaired. Likewise, cognitive abilities might be impaired because of brain trauma from events like strokes or falls.

People with cognitive disabilities may need to access computers using different tools and may be a bit slower, but many can use computers and do so. Patrons with cognitive disabilities have the same recreational and informational needs as all patrons. Following these tips when working with people with cognitive disabilities will help to ensure positive interactions.[10]

1. Talk directly to the patron using succinct and appropriate tone and vocabulary.
2. Demonstrate whenever possible the tasks you want the person to perform.
3. Break long series of instructions up into smaller sets of instructions, relaying steps one at a time.
4. Listen and be patient. Do not rush patrons as they are trying to form their thoughts.
5. Suggest age-appropriate reading materials. Know which titles in the collection provide a simpler vocabulary while still offering adult-level-interest data.

6. Provide positive reinforcement when and wherever possible.
7. Respond to questions promptly and with enthusiasm, even if it's the tenth time the person has asked the same question.

Introducing Staff to Persons with Disabilities

Theory is one approach to training, and the previously referenced ALA/ASCLA tool kit's tip sheets will help staff members feel more comfortable as they anticipate serving patrons with disabilities. However, it is through working with the actual patrons that confidence is gained. A good way for this to happen is for staff to meet potential patrons before they are expected to serve them.

Although a dog and pony show is not advised, consider asking members from the library's advisory committee to make a friendly presentation during a staff meeting. They should be allowed to tell in their own words what their needs are and how they expect the needs to be addressed. The patrons should be comfortable enough to tell who they are, what they have accomplished, and what they want to accomplish. Staff in turn should be allowed to ask questions, such as "What is your favorite movie?" Once staff members get to know that they have shared dreams, aspirations, and life-styles, they will feel comfortable and confident that they can make a difference. Likewise, they will realize that if they say something wrong, a quick but sincere apology should fix the misspeak.

Disability Awareness through Literature

Reading for pleasure sublimely allows us to learn, and why not use this approach to learning about disabilities? Many libraries and library schools hold mock juries for youth book awards such as the Newbery, the Caldecott, and the Coretta Scott King. The ALA Schneider Family Book Award could be added to this exercise. The award, established by Dr. Katherine Schneider, who is blind, recognizes youth book authors and illustrators whose work depicts the disability experience in a positive and artistic manner.[11] Dr. Schneider's goal in funding the award was to make people aware that people with disabilities are part of the community. The Schneider Family Book Award committee also maintains a bibliography of recommended titles on the subject of disabilities.[12]

If the library supports a book club for staff or patrons (or both), the organizers should always ensure that titles chosen are available in formats other than print. Seek to include adult titles that feature characters living with disabilities as well.

Staff Training in the Use of Equipment

Appoint a Coordinator

Ideally, there should be a staff person responsible for coordinating the assistive technologies the library owns. One of the coordinator's tasks should be to ensure that staff members are aware of the various equipment the library owns, know where it is located, and understand what it can do to assist patrons. The most thorough way to accomplish this is to prepare an illustrated listing of each piece of equipment and software owned (a screen shot of one application is sufficient), with information as to location and who it can help. For example, a picture of a large monitor with the software JAWS running would be printed, with the location(s) next to it, and a simple phrase underneath, such as "Will help patrons with visual, learning, or cognitive disabilities use computers and the Internet."

The coordinator would ensure that software is updated on a timely basis and that staff members receive ongoing training on all devices and that they are able to train patrons in the use of the devices. The coordinator would also research new technologies that would enable patrons and then update patrons as to the services the library offers. It is also suggested that this person be a librarian with database skills and knowledge of library science to enable a successful merging of computer science and library science.

Subscribe to Training Modules

All manufacturers of assistive software have web-based training modules; these are often basic and free of charge, but some offer more advanced training and are fee based. Some of the sessions are self-directed and can be taken as time permits, while others are instructor driven. Personnel assigned to working with technologies at a minimum should avail themselves of the basic, free training.

Third-Party Training Opportunities

Although the modules offered by the product developers are extremely useful, third-party training modules are also available, as are general introductions to assisting persons with disabilities and assistive technologies.

Division of Information Technology (DoIT), University of Wisconsin

The University of Wisconsin's Division of Information Technology, or DoIT, has a long and stellar history of being at the forefront of training and education related to making technology available to persons with disabilities. Although the school has built a library of teaching tools for its faculty in regard to web accessibility and assistive technology, the school makes the videos and podcasts available at no charge. Consider allowing staff a free hour to explore these videos and to think beyond the library's own box.[13]

Disabilities, Opportunities, Internetworking, and Technology (DO-IT), University of Washington

The University of Washington has a long history of advocacy for the rights of students with disabilities to achieve equal access to information and education. The university has always been at the cutting edge in regard to developing training modules and presentations on the subject of assistive technologies, freely sharing them with the world. DO-IT videos cover a wide variety of topics, including technology and career options for people with disabilities. These short presentations are well suited for training sessions for front-line service staff, administrators, technical support staff, people with disabilities, and their advocates.

Most of DO-IT's video presentations and publications can be copied for noncommercial, educational purposes as long as proper credit is given to the source. Others are available for a nominal charge.[14]

Closing the Gap

Closing the Gap is both a publisher of a useful journal by the same name and sponsor of a conference. Subscribers to the journal receive access to online services, which include discussion boards and the ability to seek products based on need.[15] The Closing the Gap Annual Conference invites educators, advocates, and inventors to talk about access and innovations for persons with disabilities. The fee is similar to those charged by organizations, and the conference offers attendees a chance to network with professionals outside their safety zone.

CSUN

The CSUN International Technology and Persons with Disabilities Conference celebrated its twenty-fifth anniversary in 2010.[16] The conference offers attendees the opportunity to learn about the latest technologies available for persons with disabilities as well as learn new and innovative ways to use older technologies. This is a conference that sees users and providers intermingling, sharing, and learning together. New products are often announced at this conference.

Equal Access to Software and Information (EASI)

Equal Access to Software and Information (EASI) is a web-based organization that maintains a high level of commitment to ensuring people with disabilities can access information. EASI offers courses in Barrier-Free Information Technology, Barrier-Free Web Design, Accessible Multimedia, Barrier-Free E-learning, and a course called Train the Trainer. Some of the classes are free of charge; others are fee based. Staff can opt to take courses for credit if they are necessary for their advancement. The EASI webinars use interactive voice chats and can be directed to individual or group lessons and are transcribed for participants who are deaf.[17]

ATTO: Assistive Technology Training Online

The University of Buffalo's School of Public Health and Public Health Professions supports ATTO: Assistive Technology Training Online. This program offers an array of online tutorials that are easy to understand and written for the beginner.[18] The tutorials cover the spectrum of assistive-technology hardware and software and even provide instructions on how to produce an electronic book in a manner that will be accessible.

Networking

Never underestimate the value of networking, as networks allow staff to ask questions of their peers and remove the feeling of working in a vacuum. The Librarians Serving Special Populations Section (LSSPS) of ASCLA offers forums for solving problems and sharing successful strategies.[19] The section offers programs at the ALA Annual Conference and networking opportunities at the Midwinter Meeting and supports discussion lists, blogs, and wikis, which can be used to find best practices.

Most state library associations also have sections or task forces that enable staff working with people with disabilities to come together in a learning environment. If your state association does not, work with the association to create one; it could be fun as well as useful.

Staff Training, Always Money Well Spent

Budgets for staff training can never be too large, as a well-educated, well-prepared, and self-confident staff is one that will serve its patrons to the level they deserve. The library should always ensure that the staff at least know the basics of each piece of equipment for assistive technology the library owns. Patrons with disabilities should never have to be told, "The person who knows how to use that isn't in today; try calling tomorrow"—that's just not good service.

Notes

1. The ALA/ASCLA tool kit "Library Accessibility: What You Need to Know" can be found at www.ala.org/ala/mgrps/divs/ascla/asclaprotools/accessibilitytipsheets/default.cfm?

2. U.S. Department of Labor—Office of Disability Employment Policy, "Communicating with and about People with Disabilities," www.dol.gov/odep/pubs/fact/comucate.htm.

3. For more information on working with patrons with low vision or blindness, see ALA/ASCLA, "Library Accessibility: What You Need to Know; Accessibility for Patrons with Low-Vision or Blindness," at www.ala.org/ala/mgrps/divs/ascla/asclaprotools/accessibilitytipsheets/tipsheets/14%20%20Vision.pdf.

4. For further information on working with patrons who are deaf or hard-of-hearing, see ALA/ASCLA, "Library Accessibility: What You Need to Know; Accessibility for Patrons Who Are Deaf or Hard of Hearing" at www.ala.org/ala/mgrps/divs/ascla/asclaprotools/accessibilitytipsheets/tipsheets/10%20Deaf%20or%20hard%20ofhe.pdf.

5. United Cerebral Palsy, "What Is the Legal Definition of a Disability?" www.ucp.org/ucp_channeldoc.cfm/1/13/12632/12632-12632/6184.

6. For additional tips for serving patrons with mobility impairments, visit ALA/ASCLA, "Library Accessibility: What You Need to Know; Accessibility for Patrons with Mobility Impairments," www.ala.org/ala/mgrps/divs/ascla/asclaprotools/accessibilitytipsheets/tipsheets/4%20Mobility%20Impairmen.pdf.

7. For further information on working with persons who have learning disabilities, see ALA/ASCLA, "Library Accessibility: What You Need to Know; Accessibility for Patrons with Learning Differences," www.ala.org/ala/mgrps/divs/ascla/asclaprotools/accessibilitytipsheets/tipsheets/2%20learning%20differenc.pdf.

8. For further information on working with patrons with autism spectrum disorders, see ALA/ASCLA, "Library Accessibility: What You Need to Know;

Accessibility for Patrons with Autism Spectrum Disorder," www.ala.org/
ala/mgrps/divs/ascla/asclaprotools/accessibilitytipsheets/tipsheets/6%20
Autism%20Spectrum.pdf; and Barbara Doyle, "Tips for Working with
Individuals Affected by Autism Spectrum Disorders," www.newhorizons.org/
spneeds/autism/doyle_communication.htm.

9. Ibid.

10. For more information on working with patrons with cognitive disabilities,
see ALA/ASCLA, "Library Accessibility: What You Need to Know;
Accessibility for Patrons with Cognitive Disabilities," www.ala.org/ala/mgrps/
divs/ascla/asclaprotools/accessibilitytipsheets/tipsheets/1%20
development%20and%20co.pdf.

11. The Schneider Family Book Awards honor an author or illustrator for a book
that emphasizes an artistic expression of the disability experience for children
and adolescent audiences. Three awards are given annually in each of the following categories: birth through grade school (ages birth to ten), middle school
(ages eleven to thirteen) and teens (ages thirteen to eighteen).

12. To learn more about the award, to view past winners, or to locate a list of
children's books about the disability experience, go to the ALA Award's
website, Schneider Family Book Award, at www.ala.org/ala/awardsgrants/
awardsrecords/schneideraward/schneiderfamily.cfm.

13. To access materials to use with staff, visit the University of Wisconsin's
(UW-Madison) Division of Information Technology (DoIT) website, at www
.doit.wisc.edu/accessibility/. In addition to tools concerning website design
and general accessibility issues, the site also hosts videos and podcasts.

14. To locate low-cost or free-of-charge training materials, visit the Washington
University website, at www.washington.edu/doit/.

15. To subscribe to the journal or find more information concerning workshops or
conferences, visit Closing the Gap, at www.closingthegap.com.

16. To learn about upcoming conferences or courses available, visit www.csun
.edu/cod/index.php.

17. Syllabi and press releases relating to seminars and course offerings may be
found at EASI's website, at http://people.rit.edu/easi/.

18. An assortment of usable training manuals can be found at the University of
Buffalo's School of Public Health and Health Professions' website, ATTO:
Assistive Technology Training Online, at http://atto.buffalo.edu.

19. To learn more about ASCLA/LSSPS or read about what the group is working
on, visit www.ala.org/ascla/lssps/.

10
Finding the Funding

It is understandable that at the very time in which libraries and other non-profit agencies need financial funding, the funding agencies themselves are facing financial shortfalls. Many funders do not touch the principal of their endowments, relying instead on investment profits made on the funds. With both long- and short-term interest rates low, money just isn't being made. Some grant makers have simply shut down. There may not be as much to distribute, but awards are still being made.[1]

Also worth noting is that private industry and government agencies are still giving grants to programs that seek to serve underserved populations. Likewise, there are charitable membership and fraternal organizations still looking for worthwhile projects to fund. It will take some work, but success is both possible and probable.

Grants

Grant Writing Isn't Just Writing

Perhaps the two best pieces of information relayed concerning grant writing are as follows: (1) you don't get funded by "chasing the money"; and (2) it takes more than "grant writing" to win grants.[2] It is necessary to chase the right money and catch it with skillful grant writing.

Grants, although time-consuming and intricate to craft, are probably the best way to get larger amounts of money. Before you start filling out the forms, though, there are certain processes that are critical to being successful in securing funds.

1. **Understand the guidelines for the award, and be sure that the library's project qualifies.** Do not waste staff time preparing the grant under the pretense that "well, this project isn't exactly what they are looking for; maybe if no one else applies, we can get it."

2. **Read, reread, and reread the instructions thoroughly.** If there is something that is not clear, take time and ask the grantor. People scoring grant applications like seeing things done correctly.

3. **Prepare a workable timetable for staff to complete the grant application, allowing time to submit the document on time.** The timetable should allow sufficient time for each part of the process. It is unfair to hand a draft of a grant to an assistant the day before it is due and say, "Please send this in by 5:00 tomorrow!" Requests for extensions for submissions are rarely granted, and some grantors see agencies paying high-priced delivery premiums as wasteful.

4. **The grant coordinator should assemble a task force of reliable staff, all assigned to respond to the portions of the grant proposal that are their strengths.** Staff proficient in word processing, spreadsheet development, and proofreading should be members of the team.

5. **Assemble support documentation, secure community support, and focus on the task at hand.** Although difficult to do in a library environment, focus attention on the grant until it is completed.

The Actual Application Process

Successful grant writers advise applicants that a well-written proposal is a key factor in the grant maker's decision process. They advise hopefuls to write well, using proper sentence structure, grammar, and spelling (do not rely on spell-check, as it will allow for embarrassing misspellings). Use correct terminology when referencing the groups of people the library wishes to serve, using "people first" language. Always present the facts and do not embellish, as most people reading grants can recognize this tendency and will be suspicious of other content of the application.[3] Use reliable databases for statistics; the numbers will probably be higher than staff estimates. Relay why the library's proposal is unique, interesting, and needed. The terms *underserved, limited accessibility,* and *digital divide* are still appropriate terms to use when discussing projects involving persons with disabilities. State exactly how the money will be spent and how the proposal fits the grant maker's ideals.

Throughout the proposal, always provide answers to identified problems that the project will solve. Always base answers on the library's experience and the staff's ability, logic, and imagination. Indicate how these traits will enable the project to make a difference. Grant makers do not want to fund history; they want to help make history.

Be sure the grant proposal includes information on the feasibility, community needs, funds needed, and the library's accountability record. Remember, the grant maker does not know the library and will only have the form in front of him or her to learn about the library.

When submitting the grant, be sure all attachments and requested support documents are included. Grant makers rarely contact the applicant for missing pieces; they will simply move on to the next complete submission.

The Cover Letter and Cover Sheet

Often neglected, but critically important to the grant process, are the cover letter and the cover sheet that will accompany the grant. These two items are often the last items prepared and more times than not are done from rote and are not given enough planning. Remember, however, that these items are the first documents seen by the grant maker.

The cover letter should offer a snapshot of the organization, the reason why the library is applying for the grant, and the amount the library is requesting. Use a few sentences to highlight how the library's mission and vision match those of the grant maker. If the library cannot demonstrate this, then they should not be looking at this funder for the money.

The cover sheet is separate from the cover letter; it offers a summary of the key information provided in the grant application. This document can convince the grant maker to read your library's proposal with a positive outlook (or not). The information included should present a clear, concise summary of the visual framework for the proposed project; the applicant's contact information; the purpose of the funding request; the need or problem; objectives; methods; the total project cost; and the amount requested.[4] Although this is a tall order for a half page of information, remember that your library's grant request may be one of one hundred that is in the consideration box; and you want it left in that box.

Which Library? Defining the Applicant

Although the library community knows who the library is, what its mission is, and what its vision is, the grant maker does not. In a community where there is more than one large library system, the libraries are often misidentified by patrons and the media. It is the grant writer's job to tell the grant maker which library system it is. By doing that, the grant writer can identify the socioeconomic status of the patrons, the relationship of the library to these patrons, its community-based support, and its importance within this community.

A brief summary of the library's history, mission, and goals should be provided as well as a brief overview of current projects that the library is doing. Include statistics on costs, attendance, and impact on the community as well as pending and funded projects. Include information on general staffing and key staffing for this project. Funders need to know that there are people in place who can do the project and who will be there after the grant money is exhausted.

The grant maker should learn from the application process that the library has community partners in place, that the feasibility of the project has been carefully thought out, and that it will work. Be sure to be specific about broad goals for change, measurable objectives, and qualified outcomes.[5]

Defining and Proving the Need

State the library's needs and objectives clearly and concisely to prove that there is a significant problem that the grant money will fix. Always include the benefit to the targeted population. Describe the expected outcome of the grant in measurable terms.

It is not sufficient to reply to the question "Why is the agency applying for this grant?" with vague answers, such as "The library wants to add assistive computer equipment so all the people in the library's service area can use them" or "The library wishes to redesign the website because it is not

Section 508 compliant." Keep in mind that the people reading the grants may not know what assistive computer equipment is or what Section 508 is. The readers are not going to "Google" unfamiliar terms. They will pass on your grant and move on to one that they understand. A better way to reply to the aforementioned question follows: "There are approximately 5,000 senior citizens in the library's service area who cannot see well enough to read the displays on standard-size monitors, using conventional software. The library wishes to purchase hardware and software that will enable electronic information to be displayed as larger, easier-to-read text. This will enable these seniors to seek volunteer or employment opportunities, find and use information on entitlements, and communicate with loved ones."

Likewise, it is not sufficient to state that "the library's website is not Section 508 compliant." It is better to answer fully: "The local vision support group found that at least 100 of its members who have a visual disability and are using screen readers to access the library's website are having difficulties with the library's site as it is not properly designed. The library will recruit designers who are aware of the website accessibility concerns and produce a website that all patrons can use for work, education, and recreation, using a variety of technologies."

Crafting the Budget

Grant makers do not want to see ballpark figures in grant requests; rather, they want concrete figures, and they want them to delineate between administrative costs and program costs. Additionally, they most likely want to know which library funds will be used to carry forth the project. The budget submitted should not have costs in it that are not identified in the grant's narrative.

When working out the budget for submission, be sure to include all salaries, fringe benefits, consulting fees, training fees, equipment costs, facility operations, travel, and postage. Although the library may not be requesting that these items be funded, the library can identify these items as contributions to the project.

Also, ensure that the numbers add up. Do not assign budgetary tasks to staff who are uncomfortable working with numbers. Although spreadsheets do mathematical equations for us, the correct formulas have to be written.

When securing estimates, relay the need for the estimates to be realistic and in writing. If the library gets the grant and the numbers estimated were too high, the library will have to find ways to spend that are appropriate to the request. It is never good to have to return unused money to the grant maker, as the grantor might feel the funds could have been used by another organization. Likewise, if you do not ask for enough money to accomplish the task, you won't be able to purchase what is needed, thereby not meeting goals or expectations.

You Got the Grant (or Didn't)

If the library receives the grant, celebrate momentarily—then get to work to be sure that the project is finished on time. Follow the timetable laid out as closely as possible, and be aware that circumstances beyond the control of the library may cause delays along the way. Although these delays may not be the fault of the library, the library is the organization that ensured the funder that the project would be finished on time.

Advise staff to collect needed data for the report, starting on day one. Staff should know what to count, how often to count, and whether to record anecdotal information. Never wait till the week before a deadline to try to pull a report together for nine months' worth of work. The results will show.

If the library did not receive the grant, it is perfectly acceptable to ask why the request was not funded. Simply explain that the library wishes to learn how to craft a better proposal in the future. Most grant makers will comply and share comments with the library. Do not be offended when you see the comments. Take it as a lesson to be learned and a way to discover what the grant maker's thinking process is.

You may also ask if the grant maker would share the list of the successful applicants and their proposals. This will enable you to compare point by point the responses made and the reaction by the evaluator.

The library may also consider sending staff to grant-writing workshops or subscribing to online tutorials. These educational agencies, which are both for-profit as well as nonprofit, have knowledgeable staff whose expertise is successful grant writing. Additionally, they provide searchable databases of appropriate and current grants.[6]

Networking is also important in the grant-writing process. It never hurts to ask colleagues who win grants for help. Libraries generally are always willing to assist all who come through their doors seeking help and will not turn down a fellow librarian, even if they see them as competition for the same pot of money. In instances where they are not in competition for a specific grant, they may be willing to read your library's grant application with a critical eye and make the proposal stronger.

LSTA Grants

Library Services and Technology Act (LSTA) grants are still a good source for acquiring funds for assistive technologies. The caveat for these grants is that the library must also use its own funds along with those granted to the project.

Although LSTA funds are federal dollars (administered by the Institute of Museum and Library Services), they usually are allocated to individual libraries through state agencies. The amounts of funds available vary from state to state and are based on the population. LSTA funds focus on information access through technology, which makes them ideal for projects that increase the library's abilities to serve more people. These grants are fairly straightforward, easy to write, and do not have as much "paperwork" as other grants. They do require that the agency requesting the grant contribute funds to the project. Money has to be spent within a fixed amount of time (usually timed in with the fiscal reporting year) and must be used for the project and not general library expenditures. Take time to peruse programs that have been funded, and request assistance from the library's state funding agency for guidance in applying for a grant.[7]

Funding Other Than Grants

The adage "If you don't ask, you'll never know the answer" is true when getting money to fund projects. Sometimes all that is needed is to ask the Lions or Kiwanis Club if the club would be willing to underwrite the cost of a talking scanner or to ask the Boy Scouts or Girl Scouts to raise funds to purchase an oversize keyboard. A local business may be willing to donate the $2,000 needed to purchase an adjustable workstation. A craft store may be willing to donate task lamps. Thinking in small steps can lead to large, successful projects.

The following organizations and businesses have been known to fund projects relating to adaptive technology:

- Religious charities such as Catholic Charities, Jewish Charities of America
- Chambers of commerce

- American Federation of Teachers
- Elks, Lions, Kiwanis, Knights of Columbus
- Labor unions
- Insurance agencies
- Retailers such as Walmart and Target
- Friends of the Library

The donations from many businesses may come in the form of providing staff or equipment but may prove to be the item needed to make a project a success.

Grassroots Fund-Raising . . . Will Do Anything (Legal) for a Keyboard

When the library hosts special fund-raising events for worthy projects, such as United Way, library staff usually see good staff participation—holding bake sales, offering coffee and tea service, and so forth—to bring in much-needed dollars. When the library needs help to support projects, like a tax levy, community friends often step in to help. Consider doing similar activities to raise money for needed technologies. Hold a bake sale. Have a silent auction of donated goods or services from individuals or local merchants. Administrative staff can be "auctioned off" to shelve books for the day. These are the kinds of small acts that will be morale boosters, garner dollars, and, if the library has a good media-relations staff, generate free publicity, which can bring in additional money.

Be a Library with a Plan

The library should always have an outline at hand that can be filled in when the need and the occasion for requesting money arises. There will be times when the library might learn of a grant only a short time before it is due; having a well-defined skeletal document listing wish-list items (e.g., large monitors and screen-enlarging software for branches A, C, and E; and Boardmaker collections for the main library and branches B and G), ready to flesh out, will make for a professional and well-crafted document. The process of acquiring funding is not an easy one, but it is needed for continued growth of services.

Notes

1. The Foundation Center offers a good start with its "Reference Guide for Individuals with Disabilities." Although some grants are targeted to individuals, others are awarded to agencies providing services for individuals with disabilities. Visit http://foundationcenter.org/getstarted/guides/disabilities_indiv.html.

2. See the Grantsmanship Center, "Essential Grant Skills Workshop, What You Will Learn," at www.tgci.com/egs.shtml.

3. Non-Profit Guides, "Grantwriting Tools for Non-Profits," www.npguides.org/guide/index.html.

4. Non-Profit Guides, "Full Proposal," www.npguides.org/guide/components.htm#4.

5. Non-Profit Guides, "Guidelines," www.npguides.org/guide/index.html.

6. The Grantsmanship Center, based in California, offers grant-targeted workshops and maintains a current database, which is searchable by subject need. This is a fee-based organization, although fees for subscribing to the database are reduced if courses are taken; for more information, visit www.tgci.com/egs.shtml. The Foundation Center offers grant seekers online courses in grant writing that are reasonably priced as well as offering some courses free of charge. A database of searchable and current grants is available to members, and should the library be located near a Foundation Center library, organizations as well as individuals are welcome to use the databases on-site, free of charge. Visit http://fdncenter.org/learn/classroom/index.html. GrantStation is a for-profit online corporation that offers courses such as Writing for the Review and Developing Your Case. They maintain a searchable database; moreover, they feature some grant announcements and useful information without charge at www.grantstation.com.

7. Research the types of programs for which LSTA grants have been awarded, available at www.imls.gov/programs/programs.shtm. Your state agency website should have details, including deadlines for submission of grants.

11

We Got It—Come and Get It
(or, Marketing)

Often, libraries that revamp their virtual or physical facilities (or both) or purchase accessible equipment lament that neither the facilities nor the devices are being used at all or are being underutilized. Frequently, the reason for this is that no one knows about the added accessibility. Although some libraries have been making an effort to make their facilities more accessible, there is still a sense of disbelief among people with disabilities that they are indeed welcome into mainstream libraries and that there are resources that they can independently use. It is also important to realize that many people who become disabled with aging-related issues may not be aware of technologies that could help them—and they just give up.

It is necessary to let people know that there is something for them at the library on a regular basis, whenever possible taking a multimedia approach. It is imperative for the library to develop a well-thought-out marketing and communication plan that will sell the library's informational and recreational materials and well-trained and helpful staff to a population waiting to be served.

Mainstream Programming

Providing programming has long been a library mission. In addition to providing recreational and educational opportunities, it is an avenue for marketing. There are a variety of approaches that have been found to be successful. Intergenerational technology-themed programs that encourage family participation would reach patrons with disabilities from stroller to walker.

Programs offering storytelling, author visits, tips on living on limited funds, and cooking demonstrations have mainstream appeal. Additionally, programs that feature speakers who are coping with disabilities are always a hit.

When your staff members feel comfortable with the assistive technology, host such an event. Ensure that all the equipment is working, and have tech-savvy volunteers (patrons if possible) on hand to ensure that all questions people have will be answered. Have explanatory handouts available in usable formats for each piece of technology that is being highlighted.

Smaller programs featuring the technologies could be held throughout the year. It would be fun to demonstrate a refreshable Braille display and discuss some books about Helen Keller and ponder ways having access to this technology would have made her life different (or not).

Library Website and Newsletter

As new acquisitions such as assistive technologies become more familiar, there is a tendency for staff to think of them as "old news." Although they may indeed be old news, patrons still need to be reminded of their availability. There are always new patrons who have not heard about the assistive technologies or didn't absorb the information when they heard it previously. There are some people who are not ready to accept it when they acquire a disability and close their minds off to learning about something that may help. Their outlook may change over time, and what didn't seem relevant to them in January may be important to them in November.

Use the library's website and print newsletter to highlight equipment, software, and other services on a fairly regular basis. Relatives and friends visiting the library's website may learn something new and gladly share it with the person who needs the information. Include anecdotal stories, asking patrons who have used the products to share their experiences. Hearing stories from a peer is actually the best way to sell a product.

When communicating in the print world, however, be sure the library follows accessible presentation practices. It would be irresponsible to announce accessible initiatives using an inaccessible presentation.

Both Lighthouse International and the National Council for the Blind of Ireland offer detailed, easy-to-follow suggestions for effective print documents for persons with low vision.[1] Here are a few critical points:

1. Use a font size of at least 12 points, although a font that is at least 14 points is preferred.
2. Resist a graphic artist's desire to use the cleverest-looking font for print materials. Instead, use a font that is sans serif and solid.
3. Avoid cramming or spreading words out within the sentence and paragraph.
4. Avoid italics, underlining, and font changes within a short space on the document. It is better to **bold** the words you wish emphasized.
5. Use an average of fifteen to twenty words per sentence. Sentences that are too long or too short will tire a reader's eyes.
6. The numbers 3, 5, and 8 are often misread by people with low vision. The numbers 0 and 6 are often interchanged. Be sure when listing times that the font used is clear.
7. Color contrasts of presentations should be strong. Dark texts on light paper work well.
8. Do not use paper with gloss.

Traditional Mass Media—
Local Newspapers, Radio, and Television

The media is still a strong vehicle for catching the attention of a large amount of people; however, it is often difficult for the library to get the media's attention. Be crafty when sending out press releases in regard to the library's new technologies. Although the community news editor may not think computers with screen readers are interesting, the technology editor will. An article in the paper, in the community news section or the science section, is extremely useful.

Granting that there is a tendency to want to hit the large daily newspapers with the library's news, if there is a weekly, community-centered newspaper, advertise in it. Often these newspapers like to do human-interest stories concerning the residents. How great would it be to do one on an eighty-five-year-old grandmother with a visual impairment exchanging e-mails with her grandchildren?

A one- to two-minute feature on the evening news goes a long way in reaching a wide variety of people, but how does the library convince the media that it has a story that will catch the audience's attention? Invite news stations to adopt a piece of technology, and ask them if they would do a demonstration with the equipment. Having the local anchor team up with a screen reader such as JAWS would surely make the news at 11:00 p.m. more newsworthy. Local television and radio outlets may consider broadcasting the weather using only the output from a screen reader.

This is also the type of news public radio stations and college radio stations like to share with listeners. Do not hesitate to cultivate a relationship with hosts of the shows. They too might feature the screen reader by announcing a playlist or reading the community events calendar.

Consider sending a press release in a form other than standard print. A Braille letter will get the attention of inquiring minds (attach the print version to it) and will stand out from other press releases. Another idea might be a version of the press release being read by a synthetic voice sent as an e-mail attachment.

Intergenerational Promotion—
Senior Clubs and Parent Clubs

Senior clubs, retirement units, and parent groups are all good venues for spreading the same word about the library's increased accessibility. Although it doesn't seem that identical messages can be shared at these seemingly different membership organizations, it will work.

Senior citizens will want to learn what is available to help their grandchildren, and they will readily share the information with their families. Likewise, parent groups will be eager to learn about technologies that might help their parents or grandparents.

Places of Worship

Faith-based organizations that congregate in worship are still reliable venues to market the library's programs. Many religious organizations have purchased hearing assistive-listening devices, recorded prayer books, and hymnals in large print or Braille. They are aware of the needs of their members. Often, a few sentences in the organization's weekly bulletin or on the organization's website will reach someone who knows someone who can be aided by the equipment. Church leaders can be invited to the library to learn how they can make materials that they produce accessible.

Supermarkets, Department Stores, and Drugstores

Libraries often neglect to reach people where they can be found on a fairly regular basis, such as supermarkets, department stores, and drugstores. Ask if the library can leave some flyers in the bagging areas of these places. If the library has funds, consider buying some advertising space on pharmacy bags or inserts. Or inquire as to the cost of having coupons for a "free" equipment demonstration printed along with the receipt for customers purchasing arthritis medications.

Doctors Offices and Clinics

Some physicians feel that talking to their patients about assistive technologies puts a negative spin on their ability to heal, but most will accept the reality that they cannot fix everything. Informational pamphlets placed in waiting rooms of doctors' offices and clinics would be read and appreciated for the useful information provided.

Staff

The front-line staff need to be the library's best salespeople in regard to telling patrons about the assistive technologies. They need to be willing to offer people the assistive technology as they would a good book or movie. The staff need to be aware of longtime patrons who are aging and losing vision who would be able to continue reading if introduced to assistive technologies. Staff should never assume that everyone knows about recorded books or CCTVs. Although they may be rebuffed by patrons not ready for the items just yet, they may be the link between the technology and the person who needs it. One cannot expect a low-vision person to walk into a facility and find a CCTV on his or her own; someone needs to explain about the device and where it is located.

Word of Mouth, Including from the Mouths of Babes

"Building a buzz is an effective—and free—way to create public awareness and support" for the library's new projects.[2] Consider building a library word-of-mouth buzz by asking people to tell their friends, relatives, hairdressers, mechanics, and so forth, about the service. It is important when planning programs or introducing new technologies to get the word out to the appropriate audiences that the services are for everyone.

Word-of-mouth marketing—telling others about what's available and then asking them to tell others as well—works because it's real, it's immediate, it's honest (you are not paying people to say nice things), and it's patron driven.[3] Plus, it makes the patrons feel good, as they are sharing useful information that others can use for free.

In addition to generating a buzz about assistive technologies and programs, provide marketing materials in traditional age-appropriate levels. For example, consider developing bookmarks for youth who might have grandparents with visual impairments, relaying the technology that might help them use the Internet. Often, grandparents are more open to ideas proposed by their grandchildren rather than their children. So take the time to develop marketing tools that will encourage generational sharing.

Target Consumer Organizations

Peer support often helps people cope when they find themselves having a unique problem such as a physical disability. People organize for advocacy, commiseration, camaraderie, and to learn how they can live with whatever condition they have. Requesting to share your library's information with the following organizations is a valuable use of the library's staff and money.

American Council of the Blind (ACB)

The American Council of the Blind (ACB) is a nonprofit organization that has chapters in all states and focuses on improving the quality of life at the local and regional levels for people of all ages who are blind or visually impaired.[4] The ACB maintains a strong lobbying effort to ensure that the rights of individuals, including their right to read, are defended.

National Federation of the Blind (NFB)

The National Federation of the Blind (NFB) is a nonprofit organization comprised of "tens of thousands" of blind, visually impaired, and sighted individuals throughout the United States, with chapters in all states and Puerto Rico.[5] The NFB is a strong advocacy group that works to increase public awareness of issues regarding blindness. It supports strong information and referral services, scholarships, and technology advancements.

Hearing Loss Association of America (HLAA) and the National Association of the Deaf (NAD)

The Hearing Loss Association of America (HLAA) and the National Association of the Deaf (NAD) are membership organizations for the deaf and hearing impaired that advocate for improved communication access, research, awareness, and service delivery.[6] The organizations also work to educate members on resources available to them that will enable them to interact with their community members more easily. HLAA and NAD provide current and reliable information on their websites, both of which support message boards and chat rooms.

Veterans' Organizations

Veterans' hospitals, rehabilitation centers, and veterans' groups are excellent places to share knowledge about the library's assistive technology. The U.S. Department of Veterans Affairs does provide technology for veterans who are blind or visually impaired provided they demonstrate an ability to learn how to use the equipment through its Blind Rehabilitation Program.[7] Making a contact with the representative at the library's local veterans' hospital would help to get the word out that free training and equipment use are available in the veteran's neighborhood.

Placing flyers at the local Veterans of Foreign Wars (VFW) hall, as well as requesting to speak at a monthly meeting, would be useful. Many VFW groups have blinded veterans' interest groups, whose members are either visually impaired or blind. They meet to learn about new technologies, review entitlements, and share camaraderie, and they would appreciate knowing what the library has to offer.

Learning Disabilities Association of America (LDA)

The Learning Disabilities Association of America (LDA) was one of the first organizations to recognize that parents of children with a learning disability and adults with learning disabilities needed a mechanism to share knowledge relating to the disability. Their interest covers technology, research outcomes, and legislation for equality in education.[8]

Autism Society of America (ASA)

The Autism Society of America (ASA) is a membership organization that seeks to improve the lives of all who are affected by autism. The organization works to accomplish this by advocating for appropriate services for individuals with autism and providing the latest information regarding treatment, education, and research. The ASA has chapters in almost all of the states that meet regularly and welcome speakers to share information of interest to members.[9]

Rehabilitation Centers

Most communities support a variety of rehabilitation centers that focus on one disability and work to provide their clients with information, recreation, and therapies to enable them to improve their quality of life. These centers may focus on disabilities such as vision loss, hearing loss, or cognitive disabilities. Most would work with the library to promote the availability of new technologies to their clients.

Independent Living Centers (ILCs)

There are more than five hundred Independent Living Centers (ILCs) in the United States working to help individuals with disabilities achieve their maximum potential within their families and communities. The ILCs provide support to persons with a wide variety of disabilities and abilities. All are member driven and seek to enable members to achieve personal goals of independence. The ILCs advocate on a wide range of national, state, and local issues. Locating community resources for clients is a large part of their mission.[10]

Network of Libraries for the Blind and Physically Handicapped

The National Library Service (NLS) is a network of cooperating libraries that provide books, magazines, and other reading materials to eligible and registered readers. There is at least one library in each state, and the majority of the items they circulate are delivered by mail, although electronic delivery of books is growing. All of the libraries provide readers with newsletters that announce innovations in the service and support a website.

Many of the libraries would consider enclosing your library's flyers when sending their newsletters out or, as staffing permits, mail your flyers to their registered readers in your library's service area. They could also provide links to your library's information from their websites. NLS libraries may look to partner with local libraries on assistive-technology ventures and would appreciate local libraries marketing the NLS services.[11]

Marketing—A Never-Ending Job

Although telling the library's story is usually an easy and enjoyable task, it is also one that should never end. Staff should be encouraged to share information when and where appropriate. Carry library applications and brochures with you concerning the library's assistive technologies as situations present themselves in everyday life that can be aided by knowing where answers can be found.

Notes

1. Lighthouse International has clear examples of what works and what doesn't in regard to text, both for standard print documents as well as guidance for web documents, at www.lighthouse.org/accessibility/design/. The National Council for the Blind of Ireland offers one of the most comprehensive manuals to use to create legible documents for those with low vision: www.ncbi.ie/files/Make_It_Clear_NCBI.doc. The presentation of the manual is in itself a good example of accessible publishing.
2. Peggy Barber and Linda Wallace, "The Power of Word-of-Mouth Marketing," *American Libraries* (November 2009): 36.
3. Ibid.
4. To locate an ACB chapter in the library's service area, visit the ACB's website, at www.acb.org.
5. To locate an NFB chapter in the library's service area, visit the NFB's website, at www.nfb.org.
6. To determine if there is a Hearing Loss Association of America chapter in the library's service area, visit the website, at www.hearingloss.org. Chapter location and further information about the National Association of the Deaf can be found at www.nad.org.
7. To learn more about these programs as well as to make marketing connections, visit the U.S. Department of Veteran Affairs "Coordinated Services for Veterans Who Are Blind or Visually Impaired," at www1.va.gov/blindrehab/.
8. For more information and local contacts for the Learning Disabilities Association of America, see www.ldanatl.org.
9. To locate a chapter in the library's service area, visit the Autism Society of America home page, at www.autism-society.org/site/PageServer?pagename=asa_home.
10. The library may use the Independent Living Centers' searchable database to locate a center in the library's service area; visit www.ilusa.com/links/ilcenters.htm.
11. To locate an NLS contact in the library's service area, use the library locator, at www.loc.gov/nls/find.html.

12
Creating Avenues for Accessible Electronic Communication

Contributed by William R. Reed IV

Using electronic communication can be a very effective way of broadening and expanding upon access and contact points that patrons have with your library. Although the conventional telephone still remains one of the most popular forms of communication, the advent of many other useful tools—such as e-mail, online social networking, relay services, Voice over IP, accessible Twitter, instant messaging, blogs, and wikis—has also contributed to the many different ways patrons are interacting with their library.

Although most people use cell phones to "keep in touch" or to discuss work-related issues away from a physical office, persons with disabilities are themselves proponents of cell phones for the added access to communication and mobility. For example, a person who is visually impaired may choose to purchase a cell-phone magnifier app, which can be used to read menus in a restaurant or the call number on the spine of a book. A person who is deaf may use handheld communication devices to communicate with both those who cannot hear as well as those who can. The availability of text messaging in emergency situations has become a literal lifesaver for people who cannot speak. What is seen as a convenience for persons without disabilities is becoming a necessary part of life for those with disabilities.

E-mail (Electronic Mail)

For libraries, e-mail offers an easy way to interact with patrons having disabilities. It is a good method for those patrons to request services, ask reference questions, or pose simple questions, such as, "Does the library have the IRS 1040 available yet?" Many who work with patrons who have disabilities find e-mail one of the best, most universally accessible applications for communicating. This is the computer process persons new to the use of computers want to learn first.

E-mail provides an accessible means of electronic communication to the widest variety of computer users with disabilities. Computer users who are blind can use screen readers and refreshable Braille displays to effectively compose, read, and manage e-mail. Likewise, computer users who are deaf or hard-of-hearing find e-mail to be a comfortable and effective solution for communicating.

Granted, not every e-mail interface is accessible, and some are better than others. Many mainstream computer users like to seek out and install technologies that have a lot of bells and whistles. However, if the library wants to ensure it is enabling all persons to use e-mail, it is necessary to link them up to an e-mail system with the following:

- An accessible, fully keyboard-navigational and -operational web interface.[1]
- An e-mail manager program that is functional and accessible (i.e., users can independently set up e-mail account access and do so without payment of fees).

These two simple requirements can make the difference between access and nonaccess.

Be aware that new e-mail users still exist, and they may be uncertain if their e-mail is reaching the correct destination. A simple e-mail reply, such as "We are checking on that for you and will get back to you," will steady the anxiety ridden. Also, be aware that some people with disabilities will apologize "for bothering" staff and will explain their disability. Staff should always assure them that e-mailing questions is a way of doing business for the entire patron population.

Social Networking Websites

Social networking via websites has become an acceptable way to interact. Many organizations, commercial entities, and libraries have a presence in these communities. For participants it's a way to create mini websites for information sharing. What these social networking websites have done, however, is create barriers for those with some types of disabilities while enabling others with different disabilities easier access to friends and families. Consumer-driven organizations, as well as those who work to promote equity to daily life activities, have made strong statements in support of needing access to the websites.[2]

The barriers that are created are basically the same as those created by poor website design and thus were addressed by the World Wide Web Consortium (W3C). The W3C agreed that there are a myriad of technical problems as well as security issues. They found the actual coding of the web pages do not follow accessibility guidelines. The dynamic content of these sites are being updated faster than assistive technologies, such as screen readers, can keep updated, meaning access to the information via the keyboard is not always possible. Additionally, content is being added with such regularity that one cannot hope to fix the problems. Interestingly enough, one of the nontechnical issues W3C had is that users with disabilities, who are used to moving in small environments, may not be comfortable that they are sharing personal information with the world.[3]

It would be safe to say, based on these statements, that social networking sites like MySpace and Facebook pose a challenge to accessibility for people with visual disabilities as well as those who have a type of learning disability. However, Facebook is working together with the American Foundation for the Blind (AFB) with some degree of success to make its social networking service more accessible to users who are blind or visually impaired.[4]

Although there will no doubt always be access issues for persons with some disabilities, social networking sites are a reality. They can enable persons with disabilities such as hearing impairments or physical disabilities to mingle and interact without facing a lot of barriers. When crafting the library's entries in Facebook, follow the same guidelines as outlined for web accessibility. Facebook also provides online help for assistive-technology users and advice for creating entries to Facebook that are usable.[5]

Sorenson Video Relay Service and Web-Based Relay Services

Sorenson Video Relay Service (SVRS) is a free twenty-four-hour service for the deaf and hard-of-hearing community that enables anyone to conduct video relay calls with family, friends, or business associates. Calls are placed and received through a professional American Sign Language (ASL) interpreter via a high-speed Internet connection and Sorenson VP-200 videophone.

SVRS is for deaf and hard-of-hearing callers who use ASL to place phone calls to any hearing person. Additionally, SVRS is available for hearing users to contact deaf and hard-of-hearing persons. Video relay calls are placed over a high-speed Internet connection through an easy-to-use Sorenson videophone, such as VP-200, connected to a TV or through a personal computer equipped with a web camera and Sorenson EnVision SL software. The user who is deaf sees an ASL interpreter on his or her TV or computer monitor and signs to the interpreter, who then contacts the hearing user, who does not have a Sorenson videophone, via a standard phone line and relays the conversation between the two parties. Hearing customers can also place video relay calls to any deaf or hard-of-hearing person by simply dialing a local ten-digit number using a standard telephone.[6]

Conventional Relay Services—Just Dial 711

Although Sorenson is the respected leader in video relay services, not every person who is deaf has a home unit. As stated earlier, not all people who are deaf use ASL; additionally, there is a need for alternate communication by people who cannot speak. For this group of people, there is the option of using another format of the Telecommunications Relay Service (TRS). The option can be accessed using a web-based relay IP service or by using Text Telephone or Text Teletype (TTY/TDD). It is initiated by dialing 711.

Staff should be aware of traditional relay services that exist using the telephone system. They are used by people who are deaf or who do not sign and people who cannot speak. This technology enables them to type conversations to hearing and nonhearing persons. The relay services are used when the person they wish to talk to does not have a TTY/TDD device so they need to work through an operator who does. The relay operator has a TTY/TDD machine, reads what is written in the display window on the machine, and relays it verbally to the party being called (who can hear and speak) and likewise types back verbal responses to the user of the TTY/TDD.

When using a web-based relay system, a call is placed via computer or other web-enabled device to the IP Relay Center via the Internet. The IP Relay Center is usually accessed via a web page. The assistant at the relay center will use a voice telephone through the public-switched telephone network. Once both parties are at the web page, they are able to chat.[7]

Accessible Twitter

Twitter is a free social networking and microblogging service that enables its users to send and read messages known as tweets. Tweets are text-based posts of up to 140 characters displayed on the author's profile page and delivered to the author's subscribers, who are known as followers.[8] People use Twitter to stay connected with friends, relatives, and coworkers, allowing them to share what is happening in their world. People like Twitter because with it, information flows but doesn't have to be responded to; recipients of tweets do not have to respond to them as they do text messages or e-mail.[9]

Twitter is accessible for those using assistive technology via a different portal, Accessible Twitter.[10] The site features a simple, consistent layout and navigation that meets Web Accessibility Initiative (WAI) and Section 508 Accessibility Standards.[11] Some of the accessibility enhancements include keyboard-accessible links, large default text sizes, and high contrast, which looks clear on a wide range of screen resolutions. Additionally, there are audio cues to indicate when the character limit is reached. It uses a code that is semantic and light.[12]

When using Twitter to alert the library's patrons of special events as well as regular programming, be sure to use Accessible Twitter.

Instant Messaging

Instant messaging (IM) is a very popular communication tool for people with disabilities. IM is especially popular in the deaf and hard-of-hearing community. It is a widely used application for students and teachers at schools that have many students who are deaf.

IM is also an effective way to enable virtual reference services to become usable for patrons with visual disabilities, as text displays can be read by screen readers. For example, Ohio-based KnowItNow 24x7, one of the first and largest 24/7 online-library-supported information resources, uses Spark software to enable Ohioans with disabilities to access the statewide service in ways previously unavailable to them.[13] This offers patrons an accessible means of interacting with this service as well as opening up another channel for communication with patrons for information and service requests.

If the library has a virtual online-reference site, it should include an entryway for all to use it. Although it may not be possible to use the same doorway, IM is a way to let users with disabilities in.

Blogs

Personal journal-style web logs, or blogs, have quickly become an accepted form of communication within the general population. Blogs are being used to express personal takes on news events, product reviews, politics, or whatever else causes people to feel a need to share thoughts and ideas with the World Wide Web community.

Blogs are accessible if they are crafted correctly and use blogging software that truly provides an accessible structure to work in. Although targeted to users with visual impairments, the American Foundation for the Blind offers a few tips for creating accessible blogs.[14]

1. **Choose an accessible service.** Services that demand people wanting to respond to blogs enter a series of characters displayed only visually are not accessible. Services that demand the user fill in combo boxes without the boxes being labeled are not accessible.
2. **Describe the images on the blog accurately.** If using abbreviations, be sure they are intuitive, as screen readers will read them aloud.
3. **Avoid "Click Here" and "Image Links."** These commands do not make sense when heard and not seen.
4. **Place Blogroll (author's sidebar of his recommended blogs) on the right-hand side of the page.**
5. **Check the comment form to ensure it is labeled correctly.** The comment form should include "label for" tags, and every element of the form should have its own label.
6. **Use flexible font sizes.**
7. **Do not force links to open in new windows.** Use window openings through links. It can be disconcerting both for the user with visual impairments as well as for those with

learning and cognitive disabilities, as only the most recent screen readers alert users that a new screen is opening.

In summary, if the library's bloggers simply think about the way they are displaying information, the library is on the way to supporting an accessible blog.

Wikis

Wikis use wiki-based web software, which enables visitors to collaborate to better define issues and reach group consensus. Wiki users with disabilities who use a variety of assistive technologies face similar access barriers with this technology as they do with other electronic technologies. Most access problems encountered are solvable. For example, placing section edit links next to the section title heading on pages such as *Recent changes, History, User contributions,* or the personal *Watch list* points the person using assistive technology in the correct direction. Another point that increases accessibility is to provide one heading for every entry to allow for faster navigation and thereby increase usability.[15]

Although wikis can create problems for users with disabilities such as visual impairments, learning differences, or cognitive disabilities, they are an acceptable communication in today's culture and cannot be ignored. When the library uses them, staff should be aware to follow proper formatting.

The Great Equalizer

Electronic communication stands to be the great equalizer for the library to use when communicating with patrons who have a wide range of disabilities. Remember to think inclusively and realize that what enables one group of people to assimilate information does not enable all. Good design practices apply to all formats of communications, including electronic. Create the electronic avenues; they will be used.

Notes

1. Yahoo! still maintains a text-only search-engine web page and e-mail interface. E-mail users with disabilities can take advantage of the simplicity and ease of use of the Yahoo! mail service. To sign up for an account, go to https://edit .yahoo.com/registration?.src=fpctx&.intl=us&.done=http://www.yahoo.com/.

There is an audio assist for users who cannot see or read the validator; to use the text or mobile version of Yahoo! go to http://us.m1.yahoo.com/?tsrc=rawfront. For those looking for more features and who have some computer skills, Gmail, from Google (www.gmail.com), is usable.

2. The California Chapter of the National Federation of the Blind recognized the need for people using screen readers to have access to sites such as Facebook and MySpace and passed a resolution requesting them to work with technology experts to resolve the issue (www.nfbcal.org/nfbc/Resolution_08_02 .html). The American Foundation for the Blind identified the access issues faced by persons with visual disabilities: "Are Social Networking Sites Accessible to People with Vision Loss?" www.afb.org/Section.asp?SectionID =57&TopicID=167&DocumentID=3153.

3. Rudy Racon and Pierre Guillou, "Accessible Social Networking in Practice: The GDF-SUEZ Experience in France," www.w3.org/2008/09/msnws/papers/ GDF-SUEZ_AccessiWeb_position_paper_EN_20nov2008.pdf.

4. Robin Wauters, "Facebook Commits to Making Social Networking More Accessible for Visually Challenged Users," *TechCrunch* (April 7, 2009), www .techcrunch.com/2009/04/07/facebook-commits-to-making-social-networking -more-accessible-for-visually-challenged-users/.

5. Additional information about using Facebook with assistive technology can be found at www.facebook.com/help.php?page=440&hloc=en_US.

6. Libraries wishing to explore acquiring a Sorenson relay service should contact the company at www.sorensonvrs.com.

7. FCC Consumer and Government Affairs Bureau, "Telecommunications Relay Services," *FCC Consumer Facts,* www.fcc.gov/cgb/consumerfacts/trs.html.

8. See the Wikipedia "Twitter" definition at http://en.wikipedia.org/wiki/Twitter.

9. See "About Twitter" at http://twitter.com/about#about.

10. Accessible Twitter can be found at http://accessibletwitter.com.

11. 508Portal.com, "What Is Happening with the Twitter Project?" *TecAccess Accessibility and Disability Community Blog,* www.508portal.com/?q =taxonomy/term/846.

12. Accessible Twitter, "Features of Accessible Twitter," http://accessibletwitter .com/features.php.

13. To learn more about the KnowItNow project, visit the KnowItNow provider site, at http://provider.knowitnow.org.

14. American Foundation for the Blind, "How to Make Your Blog Accessible to Blind Readers: Quick Tips for Bloggers," www.afb.org/Section.asp?SectionID =57&TopicID=167&DocumentID=2757.

15. Wikia, "Blind Wiki:About," "Mediawiki and Accessibility," http://blind.wikia .com/wiki/Mediawiki_and_Accessibility.

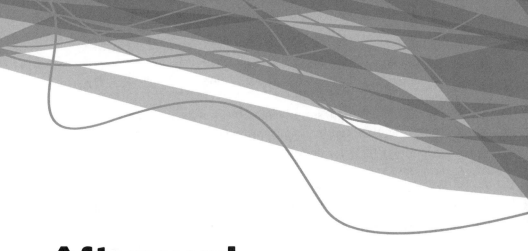

Afterword

Now What?

In an ideal world, library managers would not have problems securing sufficient funding to purchase one of everything and to hire and train staff to ensure all patrons would be able to use the library. However, library managers live in the real world. Library systems must constantly advocate for funding through grant writing, tax levies, and donations. Only with rare exceptions will libraries be able to do all that they want to do when they want to do it. So they, much like corporations and businesses, need to develop long- and short-range goals. This is a good method for expanding services to patrons with disabilities.

Start Planning Today

Although it is not possible to hand libraries a template for incorporating the technologies and practices learned, a basic plan is offered. This plan starts with the formation of an advisory committee that incorporates people with disabilities. This is the most important piece of the planning process and key to its success. Here are some guidelines:

1. Form an advisory committee consisting of potential users, care-givers, and advocates. Be deliberate in choosing the makeup of

the committee to ensure that all age groups are represented as well as all types of disabilities.

2. Assess the willingness and capabilities of front-line service staff as well as available support from staff of information technology (IT) services, financial services, human services, and the marketing departments. Success depends on staff working together to make access happen.

3. In conjunction with the advisory committee, determine what is working well for most patrons and what is causing the most problems. Promote the good; seek to remedy the bad.

4. With input from the advisory committee, determine what the library can do without any additional funds to improve services.

5. Working with the advisory committee, create a master list of technologies and services that will improve access to the library and information for as many people as possible.

6. Working with the master list, winnow it down to a realistic list and develop smaller project segments.

7. Research costs by contacting local vendors as well as Internet resources. They may be able to work with the library in regard to better pricing options, as the library will be a public show-case for these technologies. Request on-site demonstrations, and invite select advisory committee members and staff to participate in the demonstrations.

8. Determine what can be purchased with the library's budget and what will have to wait for additional funding. Prepare to write grant requests and to find additional sources for funding.

9. Consult with users before items are purchased. When making the final decision on specific software and hardware, always seek the advice of actual users and IT staff. The technology chosen should allow both to work with it in as stress-free a manner as possible.

10. Make open and continuous communications part of the plan. Alert patrons and staff of new technologies as they are added.

When crafting your library's plan, be sure to include short-term, reachable goals to help maintain a positive attitude. Do not hesitate to include long-term goals that are expensive or complex, as the library may be able to secure the funds. Events, circumstances, and community culture will make each library's plan and time frame for accomplishing specific benchmarks different.

Ten Items Libraries Should Put on the Front Burner

Librarians who act as advocates for access to information for patrons with disabilities have difficulty when asked to create a shopping list of items that libraries simply must have.[1] When asked to think in terms of real-world space and financial constraints, offer this list of ten items to include in the library's acquisition plans:

1. Support an accessible website, and purchase accessible electronic data.
2. Purchase screen-enlarging software.
3. Purchase screen-reading software and oversize monitors.
4. Enable the library's operating system's built-in accessibility attributes to be activated.
5. Purchase a collection of low-cost alternate input devices, such as trackballs, joysticks, and touch screens.
6. Purchase portable high-end magnifying devices (e.g., CCTVs).
7. Purchase assistive-listening devices and acquire a video relay system.
8. Purchase task lighting for workstations and work to reduce glare.
9. Purchase an adjustable worktable that can be raised or lowered depending on need.

and most important

10. Invest in training the library's staff. Ensure that staff know how to work with patrons with disabilities; that staff know how to use the equipment; that communications are always made in a respectful and accessible format; that staff are knowledgeable and know where to refer patrons for more assistance when the library cannot serve their needs.

Although this list is a "Post-it" note of a well-thought-out accessibility plan, it comprises items and concepts that are used by library staff who are in the field. For a glimpse of what some librarians have done for their patrons, visit the web extra page at www.ala.org/editions/extras/mates10702.

Do Patrons Really Use the Technologies?

Well-meaning library administrators often ask, "Do people really use items like screen readers?" This question could simply be answered as *yes!* But, a few anecdotes are shared:

Max E., an octogenarian, was blinded during the Holocaust. Max uses JAWS daily to communicate with friends and keep current by reading news stories and product reviews. He also uses JAWS with word-processing programs to compose memoirs and speeches regarding the Holocaust. Although he initially resisted learning how to use JAWS, his first experience in sending and receiving e-mail made him realize he needed to learn how to use the computer technologies available to him. He learned most of what he knows from William R. Reed IV, who contributed to this book. Max's presence in cyberspace allowed personnel in Europe organizing a Holocaust forum to find him and invite him to speak. He accepted and used JAWS to compose his talk and took Playaways to listen to on the plane. Max is also an avid reader, borrowing books on cartridge and tape as well as downloading titles from both the NLS and OverDrive websites. He is also a member of an online book club that uses accessible chat technology.

Irwin Hott is a baby boomer who graciously proofread a few chapters of this work for technical correctness using JAWS. He is never without access to some type of electronic tool. He administers Newsreel, a news service for people who are visually impaired or blind, and also works as a technical specialist for Universal Low Vision Aids. Irwin is well versed in mainstream technologies as they are invented, as he subscribes to discussion lists and blogs. If there is a problem with a computer, he can probably fix it. He frequently serves as a speaker at library events, encouraging others to embrace technology.

Candace R., who is in her twenties, uses scanning technology and JAWS to read lessons assigned to her in her quest to become a minister. She has a learning disability, but technology is enabling her to keep current with her curriculum.

Students of the Ohio State School for the Blind (OSSB), located in Columbus, Ohio, use accessible chat room technology, hosted by the Ohio Library for the Blind and Physically Disabled, in Cleveland, Ohio, to discuss books with librarians in Cleveland as well as with students at similar schools in Mississippi and Massachusetts. In addition to being blind, some students also have disabilities such as autism and selective nonspeaking disorders. When discussing the book *How the Grinch Stole Christmas,* one student with such a disability, without hesitation, approached the computer's microphone at OSSB to defend the Grinch's dog, Max.

Orene Anthony is a radio show host and an avid reader. Orene listens to books provided by the National Library Service, participates in the library's online book discussion groups, and writes poetry. A few years ago, she was asked to write a poem for a library event called "Family Fun and Learning Day," which brought in patrons from many places and life situations. Her poem, which follows, entitled "SOME Difference," embodies the reasons why libraries should seek to make the accommodations to include all patrons in their mission.

SOME Difference
SOME—
"hear" the lightning flash
"see" the thunder roar
"taste" what cannot be savored
"touch" what most ignore

SOME—
amble tortoise-like determined to proceed

SOME—
maneuver wheeled chariots with
blazingly fast speed

SOME—

complexions vary widely and form a rainbow hue

SOME—

tinged with melanin

SOME—

ebony imbued

short or stocky, lean or tall

denying forever; "One size fits all!"

SOME—

shout silently—still waiting to be heard

or mutter or murmur or bellow

the yet inaudible word,

Whatever,

the color, shape or size

how one speaks, laughs or cries

Whether:

"Walking" with wheels

"Hearing" through sight

"Seeing" by touch

Differences unite.

The wise know—

Difference is a prize

It's the power to change

and the ability to rise.

Note

1. The librarians belong to the ALA/ASCLA/LSSPS sections and participate in forums such as Library Services to Patrons Who Are Deaf, Library Services to Patrons Who Are Impaired and Elderly, Library Services to Patrons Who Are Blind and Visually Impaired, and Library Services to Patrons. A newly formed discussion group meets to discuss access issues for patrons with learning and cognitive disabilities as well as services for patrons with autism spectrum disorders.

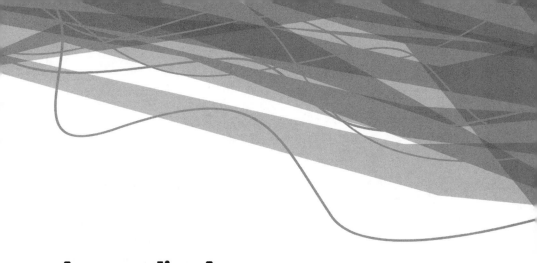

Appendix A
Vendors

ABiSee
77 Powdermill Road
Acton, MA 01720
Phone: 800-681-5909
Website: www.abisee.com

Produces and distributes easy-to-use stand-alone reading machines.

AbleLink Technologies
618 North Nevada
Colorado Springs, CO 80903
Phone: 719-592-0347
Website: www.ablelinktech.com

Company supports technologies for persons with cognitive disabilities with goal of enabling them to be independent.

AbleNet
2808 N. Fairview Avenue
Roseville, MN 55113
Phone: 651-294-2200, 800-322-0956
Website: www.ablenetinc.com

Distributor of a wide variety of keyboard alternatives.

Ai Squared
P.O. Box 669
Manchester Center, VT 05255
Phone: 802-362-3612, 800-859-0270
Website: www.aisquared.com

ZoomText screen-enlarging software.

Alva. *See Synapse Adaptive*

American Printing House for the Blind (APH)

1839 Frankfort Avenue
P.O. Box 6085
Louisville, KY 40206-0085
Phone: 502-895-2405,
800-223-1839
Website: www.aph.org

Technologies for persons with disabilities related to blindness and visual impairments.

American Thermoform Corporation

1758 Brackett Street
La Verne, CA 91750
Phone: 909-593-6711,
800-331-3676
Website: www.Americanthermoform
.com

Distributors of Braille paper and embossers.

BigKeys Company

P.O. Box 1888
Huntersville, NC 28078
Phone: 704-875-3293,
800-249-5397
Website: www.bigkeys.com

Producer of an oversize keyboard.

Blazie Engineering. *See also Freedom Scientific Inc.*

Canada House
272 Field End Road
Eastcote
Middlesex

HA4 9NA
United Kingdom
Phone: 020 8582 0450
Website: www.blazie.co.uk/
products/brailleprinting/

This UK-based company, a Freedom Scientific partner, provides training in the use of assistive technologies in both network settings and individual user settings.

Bookshare/Benetech Initiative

480 S. California Avenue, Suite 201
Palo Alto, CA 94306-1609
Phone: 650-644-3400
Website: www.bookshare.org

Bookshare is an organization that makes electronic text of books (both current and out of print), magazines, and newspapers available to qualified persons who cannot read standard print. Payment of a membership fee is required to use the vast library.

Canadian National Institute for the Blind (CNIB) Library

1929 Bayview Avenue
Toronto, ON M4G 3E8
Canada
Phone: 416-486-250, ext. 7520;
800-268-8818
Website: www.cnib.ca/en/services/
library/Default.aspx

Provides registered patrons with recorded and Braille materials including newspapers and magazines. The library also offers online services such as a secure children's chat room.

Chester Creek

205 W. 2nd Street, Suite 130
Duluth, MN 55802
Phone: 218-722-1837,
888-214-5450
Website: www.chestercreektech
.com

Source for alternative keyboards and mice.

Cirque Corporation

2463 S. 3850 W, Suite A
Salt Lake City, UT 84120
Phone: 801-467-1100,
800-454-3375
Website: www.cirque.com

Developers of mouse touch pads that can be used with gesture motions.

Clarity Technology

6776 Preston Avenue, Suite B
Livermore, CA 94551
Phone: 925-449-2000
Website: http://getwinzoom.com

Developer and distributor of WinZoom as well as other reasonably priced portable magnifying devices.

Clearly Superior Technologies

1044 Pioneer Way, Suite F
El Cajon, CA 92020
Phone: 619-579-1762

Website: www.clearlysuperiortech
.com

Produces laser trackball, as well as other pointing devices.

Dancing Dots Braille Music Technology

P.O. Box 927
Valley Forge, PA 19482-0927
Phone: 610-783-6692
Website: www.DancingDots.com

Dancing Dots provides software-translation software for musical notations, enabling Braille users to read musical scores.

Deafmall.com

Website: www.deafmall.net/
technology/

A website developed to provide connectivity for persons who are deaf as well as those seeking information about resources for persons who are deaf. Although Deafmall.com does not directly vend technology, a page of links to vendors is provided.

Dolphin Computer Access Inc. (U.S. and Canada)

231 Clarksville Road, Suite 3
Princeton Junction, NJ 08550
Phone: 609-803-2172,
866-797-5921
Website: www.yourdolphin.com

Dolphin Computer Access produces a wide range of assistive technologies for persons who are blind and physically impaired including screen readers and screen-enlarging software.

Don Johnston Inc.
26799 W. Commerce Drive
Volo, IL 60073
Phone: 847-740-0749,
800-999-4660
Website: www.donjohnston.com

Distributor of a wide variety of assistive technologies for a wide variety of disabilities.

Dragon Naturally Speaking.
See Nuance Systems

Duxbury Systems Inc.
270 Littleton Road, Unit 6,
Westford, MA 01886-3523
Phone: 978-692-3000
Website: www.duxburysystems
.com

Resource for Braille translating software. To see a well-crafted website, view all products available.

EnableMart
Manufacturers Resource
Network Inc.
5353 South 960 E, Suite 200
Salt Lake City, UT 84117
Phone: 888-640-1999
Website: www.enablemart.com

Internet-based company that sells technologies that have the potential to help people with visual,

cognitive, hearing, learning, and physical disabilities. Also sells "ready-to-go" access stations.

Enabling Technologies
1601 NE Braille Place
Jensen Beach, FL 34957
Phone: 772-225-3687,
800-777-3687
E-mail: info@brailler.com
Website: www.brailler.com

Braille embossers, paper, and other associated products.

Enhanced Vision
5882 Machine Drive
Huntington Beach, CA 92649
Phone: 888-811-3161
Website: www.enhancedvision
.com

Enhanced Vision develops and distributes high-quality portable magnifying equipment designed to enable users with low vision to travel and work independently. The website offers visitors links to possible funding agencies.

Freedom Scientific Inc.
11800 31st Court N
St. Petersburg, FL 33716
Phone: 727-803-8000,
800-444-4443
Website: www.freedomscientific
.com

Offers a full suite of screen-reading and screen-enlarging technologies.

GW Micro Inc.

725 Airport N. Office Park
Fort Wayne, IN 46825
Phone: 260-489-3671
Website: www.gwmicro.com

Manufacturer of Window-Eyes screen-reading software and PDA-type appliances for users with visual impairments.

Harris Communications

15155 Technology Drive
Eden Prairie, MN 55344
Phone: 800-825-6758
TTY: 800-825-9187
Phone (Direct VP): 866-384-3147, 866-789-3468
Fax: 952-906-1099
Website: www.harriscomm.com

A resource for information and products useful for persons who are deaf or hard-of-hearing or who have some type of oral communication disability.

Hooleon

411 South 6th Street, Building B
Cottonwood, AZ 86326
Phone: 800-937-1337
Website: www.hooleon.com

Manufacturer and distributor of a wide variety of keyboards, large-print key tops, Braille key tops, and key stoppers.

HumanWare

175 Mason Circle
Concord, CA 94520
Phone: 925-680-7100, 800-722-3393
Website: www.humanware.com

Offers a full suite of screen-reading and screen-enlarging technologies.

iCommunicator

Phone: 718-965-8600
Website: www.icommunicator
.com/productinfo/

A division of PPR, iCommunicator produces software that translates in real time: speech-to-text, speech-to-text in sign language, and speech-to-text in a computer-generated voice, which enables persons who are deaf more independence in a hearing environment. It is not meant to replace a qualified sign language interpreter.

In Touch Systems

11 Westview Road
Spring Valley, NY 10977
Phone: 845-354-7431, 800-332-6244
Website: www.magicwandkeyboard
.com

Resource for a dependable miniature keyboard.

INCAP

Bauschlotter Str. 62
75177 Pforzheim
Germany
Phone: +49 (7231) 9463-15
Fax: +49 (7231) 9463-50
Website: www.incap.de

Manufacturer of the ergonomically designed Senior Mouse, links to worldwide distributors can be located on the website.

Index Braille

Hantverksvägen 20
954 23 Gammelstad
Sweden
Phone: +46 920 20 30 80
Fax: +46 920 20 30 85
Website: www.indexbraille.com

Producer of Braille embossers, including the world's most widely sold double-sided embosser, the Index Basic D.

Infogrip Inc.

1794 E. Main Street
Ventura, CA 93001
Phone: 805-652-0770,
800-397-0921
Fax: 805-652-0880
Website: www.infogrip.com

Resources for a variety of useful alternative input devices.

Innovation Management Group Inc. (IMG)

179 Niblick Road, #454

Paso Robles, CA 93446
Phone: 800-889-0987
Website: www.imgpresents.com

In addition to the On-Screen Keyboard product, Innovation Management Group also distributes unique mice and board-making devices.

IntelliTools, a Cambium Learning Technologies Company

4185 Salazar Way
Frederick, CO 80504
Phone: 303-651-2829
Website: http://intellitools.com/about/contact.aspx

Vendor of IntelliKeys suite. Website includes information on applying for grants and some possible resources.

Interpretype

3301 Brighton-Henrietta Town Line Road
Rochester, NY 14623
Phone: 585-272-1155,
877-345-3182
TTY/Fax: 585-272-1434
Website: www.interpretype.com

Communication devices for persons who are deaf.

Kensington Computer Products Group

333 Twin Dolphin Drive,
Sixth Floor

Redwood Shores, CA 94065

Phone: 800-235-6708

Website: http://us.kensington.com/
html/2200.html

*Vendor of high-quality trackballs
and mice at reasonable prices.*

Key Connection

4600 S. Genesis Drive

Cottonwood, AZ 86326

Phone: 800-870-1369,

928-340-3435

Website: www.keyconnection.com

*Large-print keyboards and large-
print, high-contrast key-top labels.*

Keysonic

Information at www.keysonic.de/
pages/keyboards/ACK_109_EL/Action
_Keys_Ack_109EL_UK_mini.pdf

*Keysonic is an ultrasmall keyboard
that can fit in a shirt pocket, ideal
for users who cannot easily move
their fingers across a large keyboard. The product is produced
by MaxPoint Handelsgesellschaft
mbH, a German company. The keyboard can be purchased in North
America from Amazon.com.*

Kindle

Information at www.Amazon.com

*An Amazon proprietary reading
device that allows users to download digital media.*

Kurzweil Education Systems Inc.

24 Prime Parkway, Suite 303

Natick, MA 01760

Phone: 303-651-2829

Website: www.kurzweiledu.com

*Assistive technologies that enable
users who have learning disabilities and cognitive disabilities and
those who have visual impairment
to use and comprehend information located via the computer.*

Laureate Learning Systems Inc.

110 E. Spring Street

Winooski, VT 05404

Phone: 802-655-4755,

800-562-6801

Website: www.LaureateLearning
.com

*Offers more than fifty computer
programs for individuals with
autism spectrum disorders (ASDs),
language impairments, developmental disabilities, Down syndrome, aphasia, and traumatic
brain injury.*

LS&S Group (Learning Sight and Sound Group)

145 River Rock Drive

Buffalo, NY 14207

Phone: 800-468-4789

Website: www.lssproducts.com

*Web- and catalog-based company
that sells technologies for persons*

with visual, hearing, and physical disabilities.

Lynx Browser
Website only contact: http://lynx
.isc.org/current/

Although it is not as popular as it once was, Lynx is a text browser still used by some users of assistive technologies to navigate to the World Wide Web.

Madentec
4664 99th Street
Edmonton, AB T6E 5H5
Canada
Phone: 780-450-8926,
877-623-3682
Website: www.madentec.com

Resource for head tracker as well as a broad range of devices that enable persons with physical disabilities to access computers.

Magnifiers and More
7775 Mentor Avenue
Mentor, OH 44060
Phone: 440-946-3363
Website: www.magnifiersandmore.net

A vendor of a wide range of electronic CCTV magnifiers, alternate mice, and alternate keyboards.

MaxiAids.com
42 Executive Boulevard
Farmingdale, NY 11735
Phone: 800-428-6673

Website: www.maxiaids.com

Web- and catalog-based company that sells technologies for persons with visual, hearing, and physical disabilities.

Mayer-Johnson
2100 Wharton Street, Suite 400
Pittsburgh, PA 15203
Phone: 866-DYNAVOX (396-2869)
Website: www.dynavoxtech.com

Manufacturer of speech-generating devices and symbol-adapted special-education software used to assist individuals in overcoming their speech, language, and learning challenges.

National Library Service for the Blind and Physically Handicapped
Library of Congress
Washington, DC 20542
Phone: 202-707-5100
To locate closest cooperating library: www.loc.gov/nls/find.html
Website: www.loc.gov/nls/

A unit of the Library of Congress, the National Library Service for the Blind and Physically Handicapped, with the cooperation of a vast network of libraries, loans a wide variety of audio and Braille materials to qualified U.S. citizens. It additionally provides playback equipment for all audio recordings.

NaturalSoft Ltd.

6300 Birch Street, #7
Richmond, BC, V6Y 4K3
Canada
Fax: 604-261-9720
Website: www.naturalreaders.com

NaturalSoft offers low-cost (under $100) to no-cost options for text-to-speech users. Visit the website to determine which option suits the library's needs.

Nuance Systems (Dragon Naturally Speaking)

1 Wayside Road
Burlington, MA 01803
Phone: 800-654-1187
Website: www.nuance.com

Nuance Systems' Dragon Naturally Speaking provides users with a method to access computer functions with voice commands. The speech-recognition software is incorporated, in part, by many commercial entities using speech recognition to move through service menus.

NVDA (NonVisual Desktop Access)

Website only contact: www
.nvda-project.org

Free and open-source screen-reading software.

Online Programming for All Libraries (OPAL)

TAP Information Services
6106 S. Stillhouse Road
Oak Grove, MO 64075
Phone: 816-616-6746
Website: www.opal-online.org

OPAL provides libraries and other nonprofit organizations with low-priced and accessible online meeting space that can be used for programming, workshops, and training.

Open Source Magnifying Glass (Virtual Magnifying Glass)

Website only contact:
http://magnifier.sourceforge
.net/#opensource

Open Source Magnifying Glass is available free of charge at this website.

Optelec

3030 Enterprise Court, Suite C
Vista, CA 92081-8358
Phone: 800-826-4200, 800-826-4200
Website: www.optelec.com

Optelec produces a line of high-quality video magnifiers for people with low vision.

OverDrive Inc.

Valley Tech Center, Suite N
8555 Sweet Valley Drive
Cleveland, OH 44125
Phone: 216-573-6886
Website: www.overdrive.com

Overdrive provides libraries with the infrastructure to circulate digital audiobooks, e-books, music, and video. The company has support for patrons using assistive technology and is committed to providing accessible services for patrons with disabilities.

Playaway

31999 Aurora Road

Solon, OH 44139

Phone: 440-893-0808,

877-893-0808

Website: www.playawaylibrary

.com/index.cfm

The Playaway unit is a small preloaded playback device that uses an AAA battery as its power source. The unit is easy to navigate and gives the listener high-quality audio output.

Prentke Romich

1022 Heyl Road

Wooster, OH 44691

Phone: 800-262-1933

Website: www.prentrom.com

Manufacturer of products that enable persons with autism, speech disabilities, and physical disabilities to interface with computers.

Qtronix Corporation

Website only contact: www

.allproducts.com/computer/

qtronix/

Qtronix Corporation, located in Taiwan and China, manufactures a wide array of nontraditional keyboards, mice, trackballs, and joysticks that can be used by persons with physical disabilities to interface effectively with computers. Its products are available through mainstream computer vendors.

ReadHowYouWant

Christopher Stephen

P.O. Box 38

Strawberry Hills

NSW, Australia, 2016

Phone: 800-797-9277 (U.S.)

E-mail: info@readhowyouwant.com

Website: www.readhowyouwant

.com

ReadHowYouWant, an Australian company and a subsidiary of Accessible Publishing Systems Pty. Ltd., works with publishers and organizations such as libraries to provide readers with low vision or other disabilities with readable text. Using patented software, the company will, on demand, reformat any electronic document or book.

Recordings for the Blind and Dyslexic (RFB&D)

20 Roszel Road

Princeton, NJ 08540

Phone: 800-221-4792

Website: www.rfbd.org

RFB&D loans textbooks and scholarly titles to qualified students and patrons of all ages.

Riverdeep
100 Pine Street, Suite 1900
San Francisco, CA 94111
Phone: 415-659-2000
Website: http://web.riverdeep
.net/portal/page?_pageid=813,1&
dad=portal&_schema=PORTAL

A division of Houghton-Mifflin, publishing books to enable students with special needs to achieve. Website has step-by-step instructions for writing a grant proposal.

RJ Cooper and Associates Inc.
27601 Forbes Road, Suite 39
Laguna Niguel, CA 92677
Phone: 800-752-6673
Website: www.rjcooper.com

Manufactures and distributes a variety of alternative inputting devices including joysticks and keyboards.

Serotek Corporation
1128 Harmon Place, Suite 310
Minneapolis, MN 55403
Phone: 866-202-0520
Website: www.serotek.com

Manufactures assistive technologies and supports accessible online conferencing and meeting sites.

Skype Communications
Website only contact: www.skype
.com/allfeatures/videocall/

Skype allows computer users with PC video cameras and high-resolution monitors to connect with each other using both audio and video presentations. This will allow users who are deaf or hard-of-hearing or who have the ability to read lips to communicate at no cost or low cost.

Solidtek USA Inc.
5 Joanna Court, Suite D
East Brunswick, NJ 08816
Phone: 732-651-8868
Website: www.solidtekusa.com

Manufacturer of computer peripherals, including small keyboards; however, it does not have direct sales.

Sony Style
Phone: 877-865-SONY (7669)
Website: www.sonystyle.com

Sony produces several models of portable digital readers.

Sorenson Video Relay Service
4192 S. Riverboat Road
Salt Lake City, UT 84123
Phone: 801-287-9400; Videophone:
801-385-8500
Website: http://sorensonvrs.com

Provides video communication equipment and video relay services for use with persons who are deaf and use sign language as well as by people who can hear to communicate with people who are deaf.

Special Needs Computer Solutions

50 Niagara Street
St. Catharines, ON L2R 4K9
Canada
Phone: 905-641-4922, 877-724-4922
Website: www
.SpecialNeedsComputers.ca

Web-based company that sells the widest variety of technologies available for persons with visual, hearing, and physical disabilities.

Steelcase

901 44th Street SE
Grand Rapids, MI 49508
Phone: 800-333-9939
Website: www.steelcase.com

Manufactures and distributes adjustable work surfaces. Worldwide offices. If local salesperson is unfamiliar with adjustable furniture, the reference brochure can be found at www .steelcase.com/na/files/dyn/44172 3c44948523db1122f1602ad59ca/ Adjustability.pdf.

Synapse Adaptive

14 Lynn Court
San Rafael, CA 94901
Phone: 415-455-9700, 800-317-9611

Website: www.synapseadaptive.com/ alva/Alva_Pro/alva_products.htm

In addition to supporting the Alva Braille display, the company will assemble a complete ADA-compliant workstation, which takes into account most disabilities.

Texthelp Systems Inc.

100 Unicorn Park Drive
Woburn, MA 01801
Phone: 781-503-0412,
888-248-0652
Fax: 866-248-0652
E-mail: u.s.info@texthelp.com
Website: www.texthelp.com

Literacy software creators and developers of browsealoud.com and the screen-reading software Read and Write Gold for students with learning disabilities.

Traxsys Input Products

East Portway
Andover, Hampshire SP10 3LU
UK
Phone: +44 (0) 1264 3496
E-mail: sales@traxsys.com
Website: www.traxsys.com

Developers of alternate computer input devices such as trackballs and joysticks that are used by individuals who are unable to use traditional devices.

Ultratec Inc.

450 Science Drive
Madison, WI 53711
Phone: 608-238-5400
Video/TTY: 800-482-2424
Website: www.ultratec.com

Resource for aids to help persons with hearing loss.

Universal Low Vision Aids (ULVA)

8 E. Long Street, Suite 210
Columbus, OH 43215
Phone: 800-369-0347
Website: www.ulva.com

One-stop shopping for all assistive technologies for a wide range of disabilities.

ViewPlus Technologies Inc.

1853 SW Airport Avenue
Corvallis, OR 97333
Phone: 541-754-4002,
866-836-2184
Website: www.viewplus.com

Products include Braille embossers.

Web Anywhere

Website only contact: http://webanywhere.cs.washington.edu/wa.php

A free-of-charge nonvisual web interface product available from the Computer Science Department at the University of Washington.

WiViK

Prentke Romich Company
1022 Heyl Road
Wooster, OH 44691
Phone: 800-262-1933
Fax: 330-263-4829
Website: www.wivik.com.

WiViK, a product of the Prentke Romich Company, is an on-screen keyboard that allows users with physical disabilities who cannot use a traditional keyboard to access many Microsoft Windows programs by scanning the keyboard and using various pointing means to select the desired key. A word-prediction option enables some users to move more quickly.

ZYGO Industries Inc.

P.O. Box 1008
Portland, OR 97207-1008
Phone: 503-684-6006,
800-234-6006
Website: www.zygo-usa.com

Products are listed in two major categories: augmentative and alternative communication (AAC) aids, which provide voice output, and other assistive technologies (ATs), which help provide independence to individuals with physical limitations.

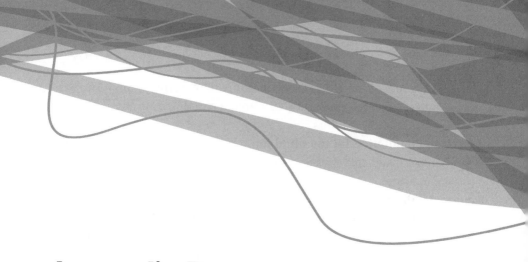

Appendix B
Additional Resources

Learn More!

ABLEDATA www.abledata.com. Database with 36,000 product listings and purchasing resources by state and country. Also, a links library addressing specific disabilities, consulting services, and individual grant assistance.

AccessIT www.washington.edu/accessit/. AccessIT is a government-funded initiative that offers an "Information Technology in Education Accessibility Checklist" and an "Accessible University Mock Site" and more. The information-rich, searchable AccessIT Knowledge Base is also supported.

Adaptive Technology Resource Centre http://atrc.utoronto.ca. A robust web resource that incorporates a glossary of assistive technologies to assist a broad cross section of persons with disabilities. Pictures of the devices and links to vendors are a part of the glossary. Includes a valuable links library on topics such as web accessibility.

Alliance for Technology Access www.ataccess.org. Works with community agencies to provide education, information and referral, and capacity building for individuals with disabilities.

Members of the alliance can participate in training opportunities and receive referrals for discounted technologies from participating vendors.

American Foundation for the Blind http://afb.org. Information, research papers, and statistics concerning persons with blindness or visual impairment.

American Library Association, Association of Specialized and Cooperative Library Agencies. "Library Accessibility: What You Need to Know" www.ala.org/ala/mgrps/divs/ascla/asclaprotools/ accessibilitytipsheets/default.cfm. Provides tip sheets that will enable staff to better interact with persons with disabilities. Also offers tip sheets for administrators and trustees.

American Library Association, Association of Specialized and Cooperative Library Agencies, Accessibility for Electronic Media. "Think Accessible before You Buy: Questions to Ask to Ensure That the Electronic Resources Your Library Plans to Purchase Are Accessible" www.ala.org/ala/mgrps/divs/ascla/asclaprotools/ thinkaccessible/default.cfm. Offers library staff a quick overview of what makes electronic information accessible. Also provides easy-to-use checklists for evaluating products.

CAST: Center for Applied Special Technologies www.cast.org. CAST is recognized for the development of universal design strategies that enable all persons to learn and achieve. Presentations and workshops conducted by staff are available.

Center for Assistive Technology http://cat.buffalo.edu. Supported by the State University of New York at Buffalo, the web resource provides information on assistive technologies and instruction in the use of the technologies.

Center for Assistive Technology and Environmental Access (CATEA) www.catea.gatech.edu. The CATEA supports a think tank for developing solutions for access needs. The CATEA network provides access to information on assistive-technology devices and services as well as other community resources for people with disabilities and the general public. Supports a comprehensive product database at http://assistivetech.net and a problem-solving wiki.

Disability and Business Technical Assistance Center (DBTAC) ADA National Network www.adata.org/services/index.html. There are ten regional ADA Centers that comprise this network. Technical-assistance specialists provide information and answer questions on employment, architectural access, effective communication, and other issues. The centers serve a variety of audiences, including employers, individuals with disabilities, government officials, business operators, architects, educators, and disability service providers. Also provides trainers and training modules in regard to access.

Disability.gov www.disability.gov. Information-rich website addressing issues such as program and building accessibility in addition to providing information on technology, laws pertaining to accessibility, and entitlements.

Easter Seals www.easterseals.com. In addition to a general focus on assisting children and older adults with disabilities, the organization has turned a focus on autism and supports an autism blog.

Equal Access to Software and Information (EASI) http://people.rit.edu/easi/. Provider of a multitude of online instructional courses relating to assistive technologies and web design. Additionally, home to podcasts and presentations on subjects such as accessibility of social networking sites, wikis, and blogs.

Family Center on Technology and Disability www.fctd.info. Fact sheets on laws governing assistive technology, PowerPoint presentations, and general information on assistive technology.

Gallaudet Research Institute http://gri.gallaudet.edu. Research projects presented that seek to enrich and empower members of the deaf community. Also presented are demographic data collected by Gallaudet.

Laureate Learning Center www.laureatelearning.com. Although a for-profit organization, the website contains useful information relating to children with disabilities.

LD Online www.ldonline.org. Website that provides information on a wide variety of learning disorders and differences and offers (among other items) information on technology solutions.

Learning Disabilities Association of America (LDA) www.ldanatl.org. Organizational member website that provides free booklets on the reading experience as well as information on applying for grants for projects that are literary in scope.

National Association of the Deaf www.nad.org. Membership organization website that enables visitors to locate local chapters and learn more about assistive technologies that help persons who are deaf or are hard-of-hearing.

National Autism Association www.nationalautismassociation.org. Membership organization website that provides links to local chapters of the organization as well as links to sites that offer additional information on the subject.

National Center for Accessible Media (NCAM) http://ncam.wgbh.org. Among other ventures, NCAM works to expand access to media for people with disabilities, and as a result, its website offers information on creating accessible multimedia websites and presentations. Also presented are free tools and examples of good practice in regard to accessible media. A list of audio-described DVDs can be found here as well.

National Center for Learning Disabilities www.ncld.org. Advocacy organization that provides useful checklists for those who work with persons who have learning disabilities as well as parents and family members.

National Dissemination Center for Children with Disabilities (NICHCY) www.nichcy.org. In addition to providing general information on disabilities, resources at this website include links to state organizations that work with persons with disabilities and a searchable database of grants awarded and available from the Office of Special Education's Discretionary Grants Department.

National Federation of the Blind (NFB) www.nfb.org. Information-rich resource for issues concerning access for persons who are blind or visually impaired. Reviews of assistive technology can be found on this website. Additionally, NFB enables print news to be accessible and has resources that can certify websites as accessible.

The Paciello Group (TPG) www.paciellogroup.com. A for-profit consulting group in the area of access for persons with disabilities. TPG's website provides visitors with links to selected resources in regard to technologies for persons with disabilities. TPG also supports an accessible blog.

Section 508 www.section508.gov. A good first stop to learn more about access to technology for persons with disabilities. Links to legislation concerning access, information on building accessible websites, and a comprehensive showcase of assistive-technology tools.

Technical Assistance Alliance for Parent Centers www.taalliance.org. A federally funded program that assists parents and caregivers of youth with disabilities. Links these people to useful organizations, resources, and programs. Also information on writing winning grant proposals.

Trace Center http://trace.wisc.edu. A longtime leader in the area of making computer, telecommunications, and information technologies more accessible to everyone, the website offers visitors large amounts of information on the subject of assistive technology and accessible website design. There are also videos available on some of the technologies. The resources are available free of charge or for a small fee.

United Cerebral Palsy (UCP) www.ucp.org. Resources regarding assistive technology for persons with physical disabilities as well as other disabilities such as visual impairments and deafness; also provides links to local chapters of UCP.

Web Accessibility Survey Site http://library.uwsp.edu/aschmetz/ Accessible/websurveys.htm. Knowledgeable survey by an authority on the subject of access to electronic data that can be consulted when purchasing electronic databases.

WebAIM (Web Accessibility in Mind) www.webaim.org. Information on creating and maintaining accessible websites as well as finding solutions to problems encountered by users of assistive technology. Great overview of screen readers found here at www .webaim.org/techniques/screenreader/.

W3C www.w3.org. The W3C was formed and continues its work on the belief that the Web should be accessible for all users. This website includes the guidelines and protocols for creating accessible websites.

Networking Opportunities

American Council of the Blind www.acb.org. Membership organization that can connect the library to persons who use assistive technology in the library's service area.

American Library Association, ASCLA, LSSPS www.ala.org/ala/ mgrps/divs/ascla/asclaourassoc/asclasections/lssps/lssps.cfm.

Opportunities to communicate and exchange ideas with practicing library staff.

ARC www.thearc.org. The Web home of ARC, a membership organization of and for people with intellectual and developmental disabilities. Links to local chapters are provided; however, membership is required for in-depth information.

Centers for Independent Living www.ilru.org/html/publications/ directory/index.html. Centers for Independent Living are consumer controlled, community based, and cross-disability. They are operated within a local community by individuals with disabilities and provide an array of independent living services.

Learning Disabilities Association of America (LDA) www.ldanatl.org. Organizational member website that provides free booklets on the reading experience as well as information on applying for grants for projects that are literary in scope.

Lions Clubs International www.lionsclubs.org. Charged by Helen Keller to become "Knights for the Blind," members provide items to libraries such as magnifiers to improve educational options for people who are blind or visually impaired. Information found on the website will help the library locate a local chapter and apply for programming grants.

National Association of the Deaf www.nad.org. Membership organization website that enables visitors to locate local chapters and learn more about assistive technologies that help persons who are deaf or are hard-of-hearing.

National Autism Association www.nationalautismassociation.org. Membership organization website that provides links to local chapters of the organization as well as links to sites that enable additional information on the subject to be located. The links page is presented both graphically and with text.

National Federation of the Blind (NFB) www.nfb.org. Information-rich resource for issues concerning access for persons who are blind or visually impaired. Reviews of assistive technology can be found on this website. Additionally, NFB enables print news to be accessible and has resources that can certify websites as accessible.

National Library Service for the Blind and Physically Handicapped www.loc.gov/nls/. Locate and talk with library staff who provide materials for patrons unable to read standard text because of a disability such as blindness, visual impairment, learning disability, or a physical impairment that makes readers unable to hold a book or turn pages.

Technical Assistance Alliance for Parent Centers www.taalliance.org. A federally funded program that assists parents and caregivers of youth with disabilities. Links these people to useful organizations, resources, and programs. Also information on writing winning grant proposals.

United Cerebral Palsy (UCP) www.ucp.org. Resources regarding assistive technology for persons with physical disabilities as well as other disabilities such as visual impairments and deafness; also provides links to local chapters of UCP.

Consulting Help

Ability Hub www.abilityhub.com. Supports a web resource that helps visitors sort through various technologies; consulting is available on request.

American Council of the Blind www.acb.org. Members who are skilled computer users can assist the library in locating and installing assistive technologies for users who have low vision or who are blind.

Carroll Center for the Blind www.carrolltech.org. Online courses are offered, and on-site experts can help find solutions to problems.

Institute for Human Centered Design www.humancentereddesign.org. For reasonable fees, answers to seemingly unsolvable access issues and universal design solutions can be garnered from the center.

National Federation of the Blind www.nfb.org. Members who are skilled computer users can assist the library in locating and installing assistive technologies for users who have low vision or who are blind.

The Paciello Group (TPG) www.paciellogroup.com. A for-profit consulting group in the area of access for persons with disabilities. TPG's website provides visitors with links to selected resources in regard to technologies for persons with disabilities. TPG also supports an accessible blog.

Usability/Accessibility Research and Consulting http://usability.msu.edu. Usability/Accessibility Research and Consulting is a department of Michigan State University. For a fee, Usability/Accessibility

Research and Consulting can help the library evaluate the design, usability, and accessibility of the library's web products to ensure that they exceed patrons' demands.

WebAIM (Web Accessibility in Mind) www.webaim.org/services/. In addition to providing a multitude of free accessibility tools, WebAIM also offers accessibility training, technical consulting services, and web accessibility validation, and it can "fix" problem websites.

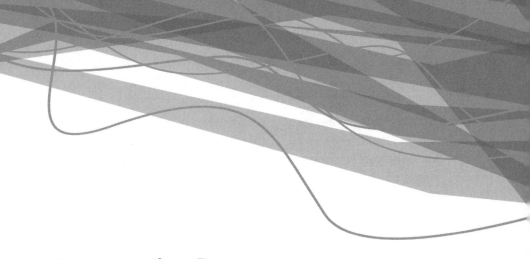

Appendix C
Grant Opportunities

Allstate Insurance www.allstate.com/foundation/funding-guidelines.aspx. Supports projects that promote tolerance, inclusion, and diversity. Also supports programs that seek to offer economic empowerment.

Circle K International http://slp.kiwanis.org/CircleK/home.aspx. Circle K International, a collegiate division of the Kiwanis Club, provides grants through its Tomorrow Fund. Grant applications and useful information on preparing grant applications are also found. The Circle K group may also be a "go-to" organization for locating volunteers to assist with training.

Dollar General www.dollargeneral.com/servingothers/Pages/GrantPrograms.aspx. Provides assistance to literacy programs that enrich communities.

Enhanced Vision www.enhancedvision.com. Enhanced Vision develops and distributes high-quality portable magnifying equipment designed to enable users with low vision to travel and work independently. The website offers visitors links to possible funding agencies.

IBM Gives www.ibm.com/ibm/ibmgives/grant/grantapp.shtml. IBM takes a multipronged approach to giving. Equipment, dollars, and staff resources are offered in support of projects that empower those who are disadvantaged.

iCommunicator www.icommunicator.com/productinfo/. iCommunicator enables effective two-way communication between persons who are deaf or hard-of-hearing, as well as persons with some type of unique communication difficulty, and those who can hear and speak.

IMLS Grants www.imls.gov/programs/programs.shtm. This federally funded program provides states with dollars for innovative programs. Consult the library's state agency for funding opportunities.

Library Service Technology Act (LSTA) has provided libraries throughout the country with much-needed financial backing to develop innovative and needed support for patrons across the country. Most LSTA funds are administrated through state library agencies. To learn about funds available in your state, contact your state agency or the Institute of Museum and Library Services (IMLS) website at www.imls.gov/programs/programs.shtm.

MetLife Foundation www.metlife.com/about/corporate-profile/ citizenship/metlife-foundation/index.html. Supports projects that promote education and accessible and inclusionary programs. The corporation also supports volunteer opportunities for its employees.

Mitsubishi Electric America Foundation (MEAF) National Grant Program www.meaf.org/grants.php. The program seeks projects that support the inclusion of young people with disabilities in society. Proposed projects should be national in scope and impact or model projects that can be replicated at multiple sites.

National Dissemination Center for Children with Disabilities (NICHCY) www.nichcy.org. Although not a granting organization, the organization's website includes links to state organizations that work with persons with disabilities and a searchable database of grants awarded and available from the Office of Special Education's Discretionary Grants Department.

P&G Grant Opportunities www.pg.com/en_US/sustainability/social _responsibility/grant_application.shtml. P&G funds projects that seek to improve lives to the betterment of the community. Also encourages employees to volunteer within communities.

Pepsi Refresh Project www.refresheverything.com/how-it-works. Pepsi accepts 1,000 "fresh" idea project submissions each month, allowing site visitors to vote on projects that should be funded. The submission process is not time-consuming, but community involvement would be a key to success.

Rehabilitation, Engineering, and Assistive Technology Association of America (RESNA) www.resna.org/content/index.php?pid=132. The fifty-six state and territory programs are funded under the Assistive Technology Act of 1998, as amended. State Assistive Technology Act programs work to improve the provision of assistive technology to individuals with disabilities of all ages through comprehensive statewide programs of technology-related assistance. Additionally, the programs support activities designed to maximize the ability of individuals with disabilities and their family members, guardians, and advocates to access and obtain assistive-technology devices and services. The website provides links to disability statistics, assistive-technology resources, and an excellent glossary, which may prove useful when writing grants.

Regional

The Hershey Company www.thehersheycompany.com/about/responsibility.asp. The Hershey Company grants are limited to areas that have a corporate presence. They are given to projects that support education, health and human services, and civic and community initiatives. Hershey encourages staff, current and retired, to volunteer with organizations that promote these initiatives.

Medtronic Foundation www.medtronic.com/foundation/programs_cl.html. The Medtronic Foundation supports human service programs that help individuals become more self-sufficient in communities in which they have a presence.

Index

Page numbers followed by *fig* indicate an illustration.

You may also be interested in

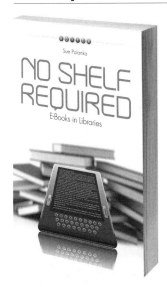

NO SHELF REQUIRED: E-BOOKS IN LIBRARIES
Edited by Sue Polanka

"The best available source for the latest information about e-books in libraries. . . . For its comprehensive coverage about a complicated topic—a theme that is so important it could help every library to survive and thrive—*No Shelf Required* should be required on every shelf." —*Epublishers Weekly*

"If you have limited or no knowledge of ebooks, read this volume. Its thorough presentation is required reading for all librarians who have or are adding e-books to their collections. Highly recommended." —*Library Journal*

ISBN: 978-0-8389-1054-2
E-BOOK: 7400-0542
PRINT/E-BOOK BUNDLE: 7700-0542
200 PGS / 6" × 9"

GADGETS AND GIZMOS
LIBRARY TECHNOLOGY REPORTS, APRIL 2010 (46:3)
JASON GRIFFEY
ISBN: 978-0-8389-5809-4

PUBLIC LIBRARY SERVICES FOR THE POOR
LESLIE EDMONDS HOLT & GLEN E. HOLT
ISBN: 978-0-8389-1050-4

BOOMERS AND BEYOND
EDITED BY PAULINE ROTHSTEIN AND DIANTHA DOW SCHULL
ISBN: 978-0-8389-1014-6

INSIDE, OUTSIDE, AND ONLINE
CHRYSTIE HILL
ISBN: 978-0-8389-0987-4

URBAN TEENS IN THE LIBRARY
EDITED BY DENISE E. AGOSTO AND SANDRA HUGHES-HASSELL
ISBN: 978-0-8389-1015-3

CUSTOMER SERVICE VIDEO ECOURSE
MINDLEADERS
ISBN: 7100-5101

Order today at **alastore.ala.org** or **866-746-7252!**
ALA Store purchases fund advocacy, awareness, and accreditation programs for library professionals worldwide.